Games, Ideas and Activities for Learning Outside the Primary Classroom

D0433410

Other titles in the series

Games, Ideas and Activities for Learning Outside the Primary Classroom

Paul Barron

Longman
is an imprint of

Harlow, England • London • New York • Boston • San Francisco • Toronto
Sydney • Tokyo • Singapore • Hong Kong • Seoul • Taipei • New Delhi
Cape Town • Madrid • Mexico City • Amsterdam • Munich • Paris • Milan

Pearson Education Limited
Edinburgh Gate
Harlow CM20 2JE
United Kingdom
Tel: +44 (0)1279 623623
Fax: +44 (0)1279 431059
Website: www.pearsoned.co.uk

First edition published in Great Britain in 2009

© Pearson Education Limited 2009

The right of Paul Barron to be identified as author of this work has
been asserted by him in accordance with the Copyright, Designs and Patents Act 1988.

ISBN: 978-1-4082-2560-8

British Library Cataloguing in Publication Data
A CIP catalogue record for this book can be obtained from the British Library

Library of Congress Cataloging in Publication Data
Barron, Paul.
  Games, ideas and activities for learning outside the primary classroom / Paul Barron.
    p. cm. -- (Classroom gems)
  ISBN 978-1-4082-2560-8 (pbk.)
  1. Education, Elementary--Activity programs. 2. Outdoor education--Activity programs.
I. Title.
LB1592.B365 2010
372.13'84--dc22
                    2009034132

10 9 8 7 6 5 4 3 2 1
13 12 11 10 09

Set by 30 in 8.5/12pt NewsGothic BT
Printed and bound in Great Britain by Henry Ling Ltd., at the Dorset Press, Dorchester, Dorset

The Publisher's policy is to use paper manufactured from sustainable forests.

Contents

Introduction

It is widely accepted that children can learn a great deal by spending time outdoors, yet evidence suggests that currently children are playing and exploring outdoors less, and not developing a connection with the environment.

Why should children learn outdoors at Primary School?

- Outdoor learning gives children freedom to learn using all of their senses and it encourages creative and imaginative thinking.
- Learning outdoors will help improve learning, attitudes and understanding inside the classroom.
- Outdoor education provides powerful learning experiences which help children to develop a sense of place and a relationship with the environment and nature.
- Outdoor learning has a noticeable positive impact upon children's confidence, self-esteem and self-control.
- Learning outdoors often involves practical, hands-on experiences, which are of great benefit to kinesthetic learners, i.e. children who learn better by doing.
- Learning outdoors is great fun for children and teachers!

Purpose

This book provides a wealth of lesson ideas, activities and games for use with children outside of the classroom. It will offer inspiration whether you are a new or an experienced teacher by suggesting practical and adaptable ideas to enrich outdoor learning in many curriculum areas. This book will provide you with new teaching tools and strategies to add to your collection. Whether you are planning a long-term project, a one-off lesson or a short activity, *Learning Outside the Primary Classroom* is ready to offer you an exciting 'gem' of an idea.

How to use this book

The ideas have been grouped into subject area chapters; however, you will find that many of the ideas cross over between subjects. The majority of the activities have a physical element, and there are many learning objectives which are implicit throughout, i.e. to develop a respect and a relationship with nature, to develop social skills and work cooperatively as a team member, to build self-confidence and self-awareness.

The book is designed with the busy teacher in mind: it is easy to navigate, the explanations are clear and brief, and the pages are well structured with an easy to follow layout. Many of the activities can be done in the school grounds and with little preparation. Visit the chapter entitled 'Outdoor Learning and Organisation' first, as the activities and suggestions here will provide the basis for your outdoor learning. Following this, activities in the other chapters could be done on an *ad hoc* basis, or in scheduled 'outdoor learning' sessions/lessons in the weekly timetable.

Each chapter is arranged with activities most suited to Key Stage 1 first (KS1), followed by those suitable for all ages (KS1/2), and finally those most suited for Key Stage 2 (KS2). These headings are only intended to be a general guide. The activities are versatile and adaptable across the age range, and many include variations which will help to differentiate the activity. Key Stage 2 teachers will find lots of useful ideas in the 'Most suitable for Key Stage 1' activities and vice versa.

Page layout

Headings indicate the subject of each activity and there is a brief description under the title to give you an idea of what is to come. The 'Aims' are linked to the National Curriculum programmes of study. 'Resources' which you will need for each activity are listed (most of the things you will need can be found in school or can be easily acquired elsewhere – visit the companion website for links to recommended resource suppliers). 'What to do' contains clear and concise instructions on how to deliver the activity as well as photographs and diagrams. 'Variations' gives alternatives, cross-curricular angles and ideas for extension and differentiation of the activity.

Companion website

Visit **http://www.pearsoned.co.uk/barron** to view/download additional images and diagrams as well as those featured in the book.

Acknowledgements

A huge thank you to Mom and Katie, for your continuing support, encouragement and patience!

Special thanks also go to the children of Luxulyan School (Cornwall), whose work has been photographed for this book, and to Jill Masters for her hard work and assistance in delivering activities and collating the children's work.

To Jack and Daisy – for reminding me every day how amazing and rewarding spending time outdoors can be.

Chapter 1
Outdoor Learning and Organisation

Learning Outdoors Safely

Learning Outdoors Safely must be a top priority. There are simple precautions you can take to ensure your children's health and well being when taking part in outdoor activities. Remember – the benefits of learning outside far outweigh the risks, so long as you follow some common sense procedures.

Suitable for

KS1, KS2

Aim

* To understand potential risks and hazards when learning outdoors.

Resources

* See below

What to do

The following is a list of points for you to consider and apply to outdoor learning situations where appropriate. It is always essential that the children understand your precautions, procedures and the rules you have developed for learning outside.

1. **Supervision** – always make sure that you have adequate adult to child ratios when working outdoors. If you are unsure about an activity, always recruit extra help. Parents/carers make excellent assistants, but you must make sure that they are fully briefed on your plans, procedures and precautions. For details on the recommended adult to child ratios check with your external visit coordinator (EVC) or contact your Local Authority. Follow your school/Local Authority guidelines on completing CRB checks for all adult helpers.

2. Numbers – you and other teaching staff should be aware of the number of children taking part in an activity, you should keep a record of which children are working with a particular adult if splitting off into groups and adults should be made aware of any children with relevant medical or behavioural conditions. A head count should be done as regularly as necessary, depending upon the nature of the activity; and there should be a contingency/plan of action for what to do if a child is missing.

3. Washing hands – teach your children that it is okay to get their hands dirty when working outdoors, but they must always wash their hands afterwards and not put dirty fingers into their mouths.

4. Eating – if working with nature objects, the children should always wash their hands before eating. Children must never eat nature objects such as berries, unless they have been directly told to do so by you.

5. Walking – when travelling on foot as a group there needs to be a clear routine, which is understood by all of the adults and children involved. Elements to consider are:
   - adults being present at the front, back and in the middle of the group
   - knowing what to do if anyone needs to stop (whistles?)
   - the procedure for crossing a road safely, blocking and stopping traffic if necessary
   - what the route will be and how long it will take.

6. Tools – if children are using tools, then the tools should be age-appropriate, well maintained, stored safely and the children should be taught how to use and carry them safely.

7. Clothing – ensure that the children are wearing suitable clothing and footwear for the type of outdoor activity that you are doing.

Outdoor Classroom

> An Outdoor Classroom is a designated space where outdoor learning and lessons can take place.

Suitable for

KS1, KS2

Outdoor classroom ideas

Each outdoor classroom will be different and unique according to the space available, the type of location and the budget. Wherever possible, an outdoor classroom should be constructed in cooperation with the children, it is important that they feel a sense of ownership in its design and construction. Insist that your children have waterproofs and wellies at school to allow you to use the outdoor classroom all year round.

Here are some features that you may wish to consider:

- **Storyteller chairs** – seats/thrones for people to sit on whilst reading to others. (See page74.)
- **Flower planters** – to add colour and scent to the area.
- **Fruit/vegetable/herb planters** – to teach children about growing and eating. (See page 164.)
- **Benches/seats/tables** – for children to sit on and work.
- **Living willow structures** – for shade and to provide play space. (See page 30.)
- **Shade/shelter** – structure built to provide shelter from sun and rain.
- **Fire pit** – a specially constructed area to house a permanent space for campfires. Only to be used under strict adult supervision. Appropriate safety precautions and risk assessments must be undertaken.
- **Nesting boxes.**
- **Animal feeders** – (See page 18.)
- **Nature area** – an area with native trees, plants and animals to be nurtured and studied.
- **Sculpture** – artwork inspired by nature and made by the children or local artists. (See Withy Sculptures on page 61.)

- **Information boards** – plaques/boards explaining the key features of the classroom and guides as to the wildlife you might see.
- **Sensory area** – boxes for containing different nature objects to explore/planters filled with plants chosen for their texture, scent or shape.
- **Play** – objects to climb on, around or through – fixed equipment designed to stimulate activity and physical development.
- **Storage** – a place to store equipment for use in the outdoor classroom.

Outdoor Kit Bag

An Outdoor Kit Bag is a holdall/backpack which carries essential/useful items to be used in your outdoor lessons. Keeping these items together and separate from the normal indoor classroom equipment helps with organisation and makes your outdoor lessons easier to prepare and deliver.

Suitable for

KS1, KS2

Aim

● To provide a collection of useful outdoor resources.

Resources

● See below

What to do

Here is a list of suggestions for the contents of your outdoor kit bag. These should be kept together in the bag at all times when not in use so that you can be sure that your kit bag is intact whenever you want to pick it up and go.

1. **Kit bag** – a large waterproof bag (holdall/backpack) to carry your equipment.
2. **First aid kit** – it is essential to carry a well stocked first aid kit when working off-site or outdoors. (Consider including spare inhalers for any children who need them.)
3. **Water** – a sealed bottle of mineral water.
4. **Liquid hand cleaner/antibacterial hand gel.**
5. **Digital camera and spare batteries.**

6. **Field-spotter guides** – multiple copies of laminated cards with pictures and names of common animals, birds, insects, plants and trees. (These can be purchased as complete sets, alternatively, download free spotter guides from the internet and laminate them.)

7. **Pencils and sharpener.**

8. **A4 paper.**

9. **Tape measure.**

10. **Mini-whiteboards** – enough for one between two. These are useful for leaning on, sitting on, placing nature objects or creatures on while studying them etc.

11. **Magnifying glasses** – use high-quality plastic lenses, enough for one between two.

12. **Bug pots/bug viewers** – clear plastic pots with holes and lids for observing mini-beasts.

13. **Whistle.**

14. **Compass.**

15. **Binoculars.**

16. **Nature logs** – for children to record their work. (See page 12.)

17. **Circle time object** – a ball, teddy, special stone etc. to be used as the microphone (the name given to any object used to signify whose turn it is to speak) in outdoor circle time sessions. (See page 140.)

Teaching Outdoors Tips

Teaching Outdoors Tips is a collection of pointers, suggestions and reminders which help to create the right kind of atmosphere in your outdoor learning lessons. There are also tips on how to develop positive attitudes towards outdoor learning in your school.

Suitable for

KS1, KS2

What are the benefits of outdoor learning?

- Enjoyment.
- Confidence and self-esteem building.
- Increase in social and environmental awareness.
- Learning new skills.
- Increase in health and fitness.
- Improvements in academic achievement.

Tips for the whole school to help develop outdoor learning:

- Recognise and actively promote the benefits which learning outdoors can have for primary school children.
- Have high expectations of what children and staff can achieve.
- Exploit cross-curricular links to make outdoor learning a regular occurrence in many of the curriculum subjects.
- Praise children's achievements in outdoor learning regularly.
- Involve parents, carers, governors and the wider community.
- Make effective partnerships and links with local outdoor/nature/environmental organisations.

Teaching tips:

- **Curiosity** – encourage the children to explore using their senses, ask questions and develop a sense of awe and wonder for nature.
- **Fun** – outdoor learning should always be fun.

- **Flexibility** – be spontaneous, react to events and discoveries, be prepared for a lesson to take a different learning path to the one which you had planned.
- **Role model** – make sure that you show your enjoyment and participate with the activities wherever possible. Be prepared to learn by referring to books and field guides.
- **Preparation** – have your outdoor kit bag ready to use at any time. (See page 6.) Ensure the children have suitable clothing and equipment such as waterproofs and sunscreen lotion, so that an opportunity is never missed.
- **Permission** – consider asking parents to sign a consent form which allows you to take the children off-site into the local area to do outdoor learning activities at any time.

The Countryside Rules

The Countryside Code is an official set of recommendations developed to help people enjoy, respect and look after the countryside. This activity encourages children to develop their own code before comparing it to the official one. This is a very worthwhile activity to complete before heading out on a trip to the countryside.

Suitable for

KS1, KS2

Aims

- To understand how to act when outdoors in the countryside.
- To understand the importance of rules and laws in society.

Resources

- Paper/card
- Paint, felt tips, crayons, stencils
- The Countryside Code poster or internet access

What to do

1. Set the activity in a context by telling a story such as this: 'I was out walking in the countryside at the weekend in . . ., the weather was sunny and there was a light breeze, it was a lovely day, but, I was almost at the end of my walk when I noticed a family walking about 200m in front of me. There was a boy, a girl, mum, dad and 2 dogs in this family – and I couldn't believe what I saw. The boy was walking right along the edge of a very steep drop, not on the path with the others, the girl was shouting and screaming at the top of her voice, dad dropped a plastic bottle on the path and mum left the gate wide open

when the sign said to leave it closed. The dogs were not on their leads and were barking at the sheep in a field.'

2. Invite the children to share their thoughts on what was wrong with the behaviour of the family in the story, and what kind of behaviour would be acceptable when in the countryside. Discuss with the children what a code of conduct is, and how it differs from rules and laws.

3. Ask the children to work in pairs and make a list of ideas for a code of conduct when present in the countryside. Encourage the children not to write a list of rules or 'Don't do . . ., don't do . . .,' but to try and write statements which promote the desired behaviour.

4. Share the ideas which the children develop and form them into one agreed code of conduct for how to act in the countryside.

5. At this point you might wish to share the fact that 'The Countryside Code' exists. You could display this on a whiteboard, or use a poster if working outdoors. Compare the code developed by the class to the official one and recognise if there are any key areas that have been overlooked in the class code. The Countryside Code can be found at: **www.countrysideaccess.gov.uk** (Look under the 'Things to Know' heading.)

6. Invite the children to turn the class Countryside Code into a poster, leaflet or flyer. You could word-process these items or make them by hand. Display some of the posters around school and reproduce the leaflets for other children or parents.

Variation

- Rather than tell a story to set the scene, you could invite some of the children to perform a role play or read from a script which acts out examples of unacceptable behaviour in the countryside.

Nature Log

Nature Log is a way of helping children to record what they have done in an outdoor session. It can be used as a type of diary to reflect or assess children's understanding of what they have learned, a place for children to complete set activities/questions or simply as a jotter where children can scribble ideas and sketches when outdoors.

Suitable for

KS1, KS2

Aims

- To sequence events and recount them in appropriate detail.
- To use a range of writing forms including poems, notes, diary etc.
- To record thoughts, ideas and observations about nature in a variety of ways.

Resources

- Nature log books (could be exercise books – A4)
- Pencils

What to do

The following are a selection of ideas for ways in which to use a nature log and some suggestions on what could be included inside.

1. **Diary** – ask the children to complete a short diary entry following every activity which you do outside. This could be in an informal style and include pictures.

2. **Journal** – allow the children to spend 10 minutes writing down their thoughts and feelings whilst sitting outdoors.

3. **Notebook** – the children can use the nature log to keep notes during activities. These could be in the form of written notes or labelled sketches.

4. **Species record** – the children record a drawing and notes about every new species of plant/animal they discover in their outdoor environment.

5. **Species spotter** – the children are given a list of different plant/animal species to stick into their nature logs. Each time they discover an item from the list, they tick it off.

6. **Observational drawing** – gather nature objects and invite the children to sketch and label them.

7. **Outdoor rules/agreement** – stick a copy of your class outdoor rules/behaviour agreement into the back of the nature log as it may be useful to refer to this whilst out and about.

Variations

- You might want to consider fixing a pencil to the spine of each child's nature log using string and sticky tape.
- You could cover the nature log cover using sticky-backed plastic to help make it more durable.

Chapter 2
Art & DT

Camping Creations

Camping Creations are useful campsite items or objects made using only sticks and string. The children will need to work together and think creatively in this challenging activity.

Suitable for

KS2

Aims

- To combine and organise a variety of materials to make artefacts.
- To assemble and join components to make objects which solve problems.
- To face new challenges positively and collaborate to find solutions.

Resources

- Large collection of sticks/twigs/canes
- String
- Empty washing up bowls and plates (optional)
- Pairs of shoes (optional)
- Torches (optional)
- Hand towels (optional)
- Fruit and vegetables (optional)

What to do

1. Divide the class into small mixed ability groups and encourage each group to choose a nature-based name. Seat the groups together in a large circle outdoors and explain: 'Your challenge today is to make a useful camping creation. This is an item or an object built from sticks and string which solves a real-life problem when camping or living outdoors.'

2. You can choose which problems you set for the children to solve depending upon their age and ability. Here are some suggestions:

- We need to keep the washing up bowl off the uneven grass and provide somewhere for the clean plates to dry. Can you solve it?
- Can you make something which will keep a torch pointing at your book when reading at night in your sleeping bag?
- My wet shoes won't dry out. Can you find a way of letting them dry out without them touching the grass?
- The wet hand towels keeping blowing away in the wind. Can you help?
- The fruit and vegetables are going to be eaten by insects if they are left on the grass. What can we do?

3. If you decide to allow children to insert sticks or canes into the ground as part of their solutions to the problems, make sure that you explain the potential hazards and decide upon some safety rules for the activity e.g., no running around the objects, carefully remove every stick/cane at the end of the activity etc. These rules should be in addition to those developed as a part of a working outdoors agreement/policy developed in collaboration with the children. It may be appropriate to have an adult working with each of the groups for this activity.

4. Encourage the children to test and adapt or improve their camping creations before the groups present their objects to the rest of the class at the end of the session.

5. You could award points to each of the groups for the successfulness of their camping creation, how well they collaborated as a group, the quality of their listening and presenting and how safely they acted through the activity.

Variations

- Why not incorporate this activity into an overnight camp or external visit?
- You could set the same camping problem for all of the groups to solve and see the different solutions that they create.
- The children could be shown how to tie some basic knots and how to lash sticks together in a focused practical task before they attempt to build their camping creations.

Animal Feeders

Animal Feeders are great to make; they are also fascinating to watch. Here are three simple and effective ideas to try. The children will need plenty of assistance and supervision when making these.

Suitable for

KS1, KS2

Aims

- To combine and organise a variety of materials to make artefacts.
- To understand that humans and other animals need food and water to stay alive.

Resources

Hanging feeding table

- Piece of plywood approx. 25 × 25cm
- Dowel rod – 4 pieces, each 23cm long
- Screw eyes/4 screws, screwdriver and 4 washers
- Hand drill/bradawl to make pilot holes
- Thick string/rope
- Sticky tape/glue gun
- Bird seed or other bird food

Bird feeder

- Empty plastic drinks bottle
- Dowel rod
- Hammer and a strong nail
- Scissors
- String/rope

Bird cake

- Empty yoghurt pot/small plastic plant pot
- Bird seed plus any food that birds will eat
- Lard
- Cooker/microwave
- Fridge
- String
- Bowls and spoons

What to do

Hanging feeding table:

1. Attach four equal lengths of thick string or rope to the corners of the piece of plywood. Do this by either fixing a screw eye to each corner, or fixing a screw through a knot in the string with a washer to clamp it down.

2. Use sticky tape or a glue gun to secure the pieces of dowel rod around the edge of the plywood table to help stop the seed from falling off.

3. Take the table outside and knot the strings together over a tree branch and add some bird seed.

Bird feeder:

1. Rinse out the empty plastic bottle. Make two pairs of holes which penetrate through the bottle using a hammer and a strong nail. Push the dowel rod pieces through the holes, leaving enough protruding on either side to act as a perch.

2. Carefully cut small holes above the perches for the birds to feed through (this may need to be done by an adult). Pour in the bird seed using a funnel if you have one. Put the top back on the bottle and use string to attach it to a tree branch.

Bird cake:

1. Have an adult melt the lard using a cooker or microwave. Pour into a bowl. Add bird seed and any other food which birds will eat and mix together well using a spoon whilst the mixture is warm.

2. Thread a knotted piece of string through a hole in the centre of a plant pot/yoghurt pot.

3. Pour in the mixture and place in a fridge to set before taking outside to attach to a tree or hedge.

Animal Masks

Animal Masks are very useful and versatile tools, which can be made as an art project and then used in a whole range of other activities and lessons to add colour and excitement.

Suitable for

KS1, KS2

Aims

- To combine and organise a variety of materials to make artefacts.
- To recognise and compare animals.

Resources

- Elastic or string to tie the masks
- Hole punch
- Self-adhesive paper reinforcement rings (optional)
- Scissors

Depending upon the type of mask being made:

- A4 card/art paper
- Mask outline printouts
- Full-colour mask printouts
- Computers with internet access
- Paints/crayons/felt tips/collage materials – fabric/feathers/paper scraps

What to do

The following are different methods of making animal masks based upon the basic technique of punching 2 holes on either side of a mask and securing the mask with a piece of elastic or string, measured to fit the child's head:

1. **Outline masks** – draw or print out from the internet an outline drawing of the chosen animal to be decorated by the children using paint, crayon or collage.

2. **Colour masks** – print out full-colour masks from the internet, or resize head shots taken from photographs of real animals and print.

3. **Half masks** – make masks which finish just below the nose, thus allowing the children to talk without any restrictions – ideal for drama activities.

4. **Clay masks** – use air drying clay to make a half face mask which can be painted once dry. Secure with elastic, remembering to make 2 strong holes in the mask on either side, before it dries.

Variations

- Use self-adhesive paper reinforcement rings to add strength to the mask and avoid the problem of them tearing when the children take them on and off.
- Make masks which are mounted onto a dowel rod or cane which can be held up in front of the child's face.
- Use the masks to add excitement to drama, dance or science activities.
- Try combining half masks with child-friendly face paints.

Kite Making

Kite Making is a practical activity which links in well with the study of forces, or is a hugely enjoyable project in its own right. Children love to decorate their kites and enjoy the challenge of getting them to fly.

Suitable for

KS1, KS2

Aims

- To combine and organise a variety of materials to make artefacts.
- To understand the forces involved which cause a kite to fly.

Resources

- Pieces of thin dowel rod or cane
- String
- Glue
- Sticky tape
- Thick paper
- Corrugated cardboard squares (approx. 12 × 12cm)
- Felt tips/paints to decorate with
- Ribbon or hazard marking tape
- Simple shop-bought kite (or homemade kite)
- Kite part labels or large post-it notes

What to do

1. Seat the class outside in a circle and invite a pair of children to fly a simple shop-bought (or homemade) kite. Emphasise the importance of teamwork and communication when trying to get the kite to fly. Discuss the dangers of flying kites near power lines, people, animals and roads. You may wish to give the children some tips on how to improve their kite flying technique.

2. Place the kite in the centre of the circle and ask individuals to place a kite part label (alternatively you could write the words on post-it notes and the children could stick them onto the kite) on the correct part of the kite. Some of the names for kite parts are as follows:

   - **Spine**: the vertical stick or backbone of the kite
   - **Spar**: the horizontal or supporting stick
   - **Flying line**: the string which goes from the hand to the kite
   - **Bridle**: the string/s attaching the flying line to the kite frame which help to control its flight.
   - **Tail**: a long strip which flies behind the kite helping with balance
   - **Reel**: an object held in the hand and used to wind in the flying line
   - **Cover/wing**: the paper, material or plastic used to cover the frame.

3. Invite the children to design and make their own kite in pairs or small groups. You may wish to ask all of the children to make the same style of kite following your instructions, alternatively, they could choose from a variety of kite templates or you could allow the children the freedom to create their own design.

4. Here are some instructions for making a simple diamond-shaped kite:

   a. Make a cross with 2 dowel rods. The spine should be 100cm long and the spar 88cm. Fix them together at right angles using string or tape.

   b. Cut and fix a single piece of string which runs all around the edge of the frame to make the outline of a diamond. Try wrapping the string tightly around each end of the dowel ends as you pass them. Finish by making a loop at the bottom of the diamond. (This is where the tail will be attached later.)

   c. Lie the frame onto a large piece of strong paper (e.g. display paper, sugar paper) and cut around the outline of the kite leaving a border of 3cm. Tape or glue this border flap down over the string to secure the cover to the frame. Decorate the cover.

   d. Make a bridle by tying a piece of string (50cm long) in 2 places on the spar, on either side of the spine. Tie a flying line to the centre of this bridle.

   e. Roll up a corrugated card square to form a tube and secure with tape. Tie the end of the flying line securely onto the tube and wrap the excess flying line around this to form a reel.

   f. Make and attach a tail using ribbon or hazard tape. Adjust the kite until it is balanced. Leave to dry and then try to fly!

Variations

- Why not turn the activity into a longer project by asking the children to design their kite based on some focused practical investigations using a variety of cover materials, shapes and designs.
- You could ask the groups to write a set of instructions on how to fly a kite safely.
- Try searching the internet for stories about kites or research the history and use of kites in China.
- For younger children, an extremely simple small kite can be made using bamboo skewers taped down with masking tape on the back of a diamond shaped piece of sugar paper. Attach a tail and flying line and they are ready to fly.

Leaf Rubbing

Leaf Rubbing is a simple and quick activity which has been enjoyed by children for many years. Try some of the variations once your children have mastered the basic method.

Suitable for

KS1, KS2

Aims

- To try out and apply tools and techniques.
- To learn the names and leaf shapes of common tree species.
- To learn the names of different leaf parts and understand their function.

Resources

- Wax crayons
- Pieces of paper
- Paper/card/whiteboards as a backing board whilst rubbing
- Leaves
- Masking tape (optional)

What to do

1. Explain and demonstrate how to do a basic leaf rubbing:
   - Take a leaf and place it on a piece of paper/card/small whiteboard on a flat surface. Make sure that the vein side is facing up.
   - Place a piece of paper on top of the leaf and secure with tape (tape is optional).
   - Take a wax crayon, turn it on its side and gently rub over the top sheet of paper.

2. Here are some variations on the basic method:

- **Leaf hunter.** Give the children 3 tree species names and ask them to find a leaf from each species and do a rubbing on one piece of paper and then label the leaves.
- **Rubbing bingo.** Give the children different bingo cards with the names of tree species and objects such as feathers, grass, bark. The first children to return with all of the rubbings completed are the winners.
- **Leaf detectives.** Ask the children to collect 3 rubbings of different leaves on a plain piece of paper. The children return to the classroom and swap sheets and use books, leaf cards or the internet to research and label the leaves on their new sheet.
- **Leafy picture.** Lay out lots of leaves in a pattern or randomly, secure them and do a rubbing. Try using different coloured crayons on the same page.
- Use an A3 size piece of paper, draw the outline of a tree and do rubbings of leaves to make the foliage and bark for the trunk.
- **Leaf parts.** After completing a simple rubbing, ask the children to label the different parts of a leaf with the correct terms:

  Blade – the flat surface of a leaf
  Stalk/petiole – the part which joins the leaf to the plant/tree
  Margin – the edge of the leaf, this can be entire, lobed or toothed
  Vein – the lines which run from the tip and edge
  Apex – the tip of the leaf.

*Why not ask older children to research what each part of the leaf does and why/how?

Living Willow Structures

Living Willow Structures are great fun to make and fascinating to watch grow. Willow can be twisted into almost any shape and children love to design and plant structures which will provide play space and shade. Living willow is beautiful, tactile and environmentally friendly.

Suitable for

KS1, KS2

Aims

- To measure, mark out, cut and shape materials.
- To assemble, combine and join components thinking about how the working characteristics of materials affect the ways they are used.
- To work collaboratively.

Resources

- Willow rods and lengths of non-living willow (These can be purchased separately or in kit form to make a tunnel, dome or fence etc. from the suppliers listed below.)
- Spades
- Tape measures
- Strong spike to make holes for the willow rods
- Marker pegs/sticks
- Bark chippings
- Compost
- Secateurs
- Watering can

What to do

1. Living willow is cut and sold between January and April. This is the best time to plant your structure. Willow rods can be kept alive in water in a dark room until they are needed. Living willow rods and kits are available from P H Coate & Son at **www.englishwillowbaskets.co.uk** or from Suzanne & Richard Kerwood at **www.windrushwillow.com**.

2. Here are some planting guidelines for a living willow dome:

    a. Mark out a circle and cut away a spade's width of turf, apart from where the entrance/doorway will be.

    b. Make holes with the spike at regular intervals in the trench you have dug. (The number of holes depends upon the quantity of willow you have.) Use a stick as a spacer between the holes to mark their position. Make 3 holes close together on either side of the entrance.

    c. Fill the holes with some water and compost.

    d. Snip off the base ends of the willow rods on a diagonal and push them into the holes holding the willow firmly near the base. Add more compost and water.

    e. Form the doorway by twisting/plaiting the 3 rods around each other on either side of the entrance, then join both sides together by twisting and secure them with string.

    f. Weave lengths of non-living willow in and around the vertical rods to make horizontal bands which will give strength and help to space out the rods.

    g. Make angled holes in between the upright rods, add water and compost, then insert rods to make a diagonal pattern. Weave the rods in and out of the uprights and secure with string.

    h. Draw the upright rods together at the top and secure with string. Spread bark chippings in the trench around the base of the rods to help suppress weeds and retain moisture. Water the willow well and then water regularly, especially during the first season. As the willow grows you can weave in the new growth to thicken the structure.

3. Living willow is extremely versatile and affordable, and you can make virtually any design that you or the children can think of, so be creative!

Variations

- Planting living willow has many strong links with Maths in terms of measuring, shapes, pattern etc. Why not build a willow structure as part of a Maths investigation? Here are some example problems:

  How many willow uprights will we need if we want to build a dome which is 2 metres in diameter?

  If we have 70 willow uprights, how far apart will they need to be spaced if we want the dome to have a diameter of 3 metres?

  What is the total length of willow needed to build our structure?

This is a living willow dome and tunnel which was built with the help of children from Key Stages 1 & 2 from Luxulyan School.

Mirror Making

Mirror Making is a fun activity and a good way to follow an outdoor walk or trip to the beach. The finished mirrors make a lovely display, if you can convince the children not to take them home!

Suitable for

KS1, KS2

Aim

- To combine and organise a variety of materials to make artefacts.

Resources

- Pieces of mirror card
- Collection of nature objects
- Glue guns/good PVA glue
- Fishing line
- Hole punch

What to do

1. Lead a walk/activity where the children can collect some nature objects. Encourage the children to choose objects that are small enough to fit along on the edge of a piece of mirror card. Take one piece of mirror card to show the children the size. You could allow younger children to check their objects for size against the example piece.

2. Return to the classroom and explain to the children: 'Look at the nature objects you have collected and then place them onto your piece of mirror card around the edge, thinking about the way that they will look. You could try to make a pattern or arrange the objects in a way that looks good. Remember to leave plenty of space in the centre of the mirror.'

3. Once the children are happy with their design, help them to stick the objects down. There are a number of ways of doing this depending on what the nature objects are:
   - Use a hot glue gun with appropriate supervision.
   - Make holes with a hole punch underneath sticks or driftwood and use fishing line to tie them down

4. Encourage the children to allow the glue to dry completely before picking up their mirror. You could invite the children to look at each other's work and make evaluative comments while the glue is drying.

Variations

- The children can make a mirror individually, in pairs, or in groups.
- Why not turn the activity into a longer project by asking the children to design their mirror first, then go out and collect specific nature objects with their design in mind. This could be a good opportunity for developing measuring skills.

Nature Collage

Nature Collage is a fantastic opportunity for children to collect materials from nature and create designs. The children will explore pattern, texture and arrangement to create an environmental work of art.

Suitable for

KS1, KS2

Aims

- To investigate and combine materials to match the purpose of the work.
- To compare methods and approaches in their own and other artists' work and say what they think and feel about them.

Resources

- Photographs of art by Andy Goldsworthy
- Collection of nature materials
- Digital camera
- Large sheets of paper

What to do

1. Display a range of photographs of artwork by Andy Goldsworthy, a British environmental artist. These can be found easily by using an internet search engine. The photographs should include works of art which are made with materials from nature.

2. Lead a discussion to identify the key features and themes of the photographs. Explain to the children: 'You are going to be creating your own nature collage. You will need to take time to carefully arrange the materials from nature into a shape or pattern which looks effective. Once you are happy with your design, you will take a photograph of it which will be printed out and displayed.'

3. The children could then go and collect materials for their nature collage such as: twigs, leaves, pine cones and seed pods. The children will need to be given clear rules on what to collect and be supervised during this collection. If there is no possibility of collecting nature materials on the school site, then a trip could be arranged to do this at a nearby park, the teacher could collect and bring in nature materials or the children could bring in materials collected at home with parental supervision.

4. Once the materials have been collected, the children can arrange them outside on a range of surfaces (grass/soil/concrete) or alternatively they can arrange their collage on large sheets of paper inside the classroom. The children should be encouraged to experiment with different arrangements before selecting their final design to be photographed.

5. The children must wash their hands after creating their collage.

Variations

- The children can create a nature collage individually, in pairs, in groups or as a whole class. Remember that the larger the collage becomes, the higher you will need to be to take a photograph!
- You may wish to give younger children a smaller selection of materials to arrange, or make a pattern for the children on paper by writing down the names of materials such as twig/leaf/cone. The children then put the appropriate object down on the name to create their collage.

This photo/image is provided by Clare Brewer, a visual artist and teacher who works in the Midlands area. She is able to provide practical art workshops based on nature themes for all of the primary age range. Contact **clarebrewer@ntlworld.com** for details.

Nature Mobile

> Nature Mobile is a good way to follow an outdoor walk or trip to the beach. The children use nature objects which they collect to make a hanging display.

Suitable for

KS1, KS2

Aims

- To combine and organise a variety of materials to make artefacts.
- To find different ways of solving balance and weight problems.

Resources

- Masking/sticky tape
- Cotton/fishing line/string
- Collection of nature objects, including sticks/twigs to hang objects from
- Scissors

What to do

1. Lead a walk/activity where the children can collect some nature objects. Encourage the children to choose objects that are small enough to be hung using a thin piece of cotton or string. Make sure that every child also collects a stick/twig which is strong and long enough to use as the bar to hang the other objects from.

2. Return to the classroom and explain to the children: 'You need to choose 4 or 5 objects from your collection which will hang from your stick. To hang them you will need to tie a piece of cotton to the object and then tie the other end to the stick. Some objects will be tricky to tie on, so you can use tape to fix the end of the string to the back of those ones. Try hanging the objects at different heights and remember

that the mobile needs to balance when it is hung up, so try moving the objects around if it doesn't balance at first.'

3. Tie a long piece of string which runs from one end of the stick/twig to the other on each mobile, and use this to hang the mobiles.

Variations

- The children could make pictures or replicas of nature objects using card or air dry clay; these can then be hung from the mobiles.
- Try using bamboo or garden canes in place of sticks and twigs.
- Why not add some drawings/paintings of any animals or insects which you saw on your walk to the nature mobiles?
- You could link this activity to a study of weights/balance or forces in Maths or Science.

Nature Photography

With many classrooms having access to digital cameras, nature photography is a great activity to engage your class. A nature walk takes on a new dimension if the children use cameras to capture the events.

Suitable for

KS1, KS2

Aims

- To improve the ability to take a photograph.
- To study small details in nature.
- To make evaluative comments on own and others' work.

Resources

- Digital cameras and spare batteries (1 between 2/3)
- Photo tricks cards (optional)
- Shot list cards (optional)
- Printer

What to do

1. Demonstrate how to use a digital camera. Explain the basic camera features/actions such as: the lens, focus, shutter, flash, macro (close-up photo tool – usually indicated by a tiny flower), turning on and off, taking a photo and camera modes. The level to which you explain the workings and features of a camera depends upon the age and ability of your children. Be aware that if the children are using different makes and models of digital camera, then the operation of each type may be different. Ideally, all children would use the same make and model of camera, but this isn't always practical.

2. Make sure that the children understand how to use the cameras and have proved that they can operate them by taking a picture and showing it to you. Ideally, the children should share a camera in pairs or in threes, taking turns to take shots. Make sure that you have the permission of parents or carers to take and use pictures of the children.

3. Choose the type of photographic expedition you want to lead:

   a. **Shot List**. Lead a walk either on a circular route or to a specific area where the children can take photos. Give each group a shot list which tells them specific photographs which you want them to take, e.g. a photo of the bridge, a close-up of a flower, a picture of your partner walking towards you, something beautiful, a landscape shot etc.

   b. **Photo tricks**. Lead a photography walk where the children refer to a photo tricks card. This is a list of tips and ideas on how to take better photographs, e.g. fit the shape of the subject by turning the camera on its side, shoot with the sun behind you or to the side, use the zoom function to capture smaller objects, check all of the frame before you shoot – move yourself or the camera to get the best shot, try getting down low to capture shots of things on the ground, hold the side of the camera close to a wall or rail and take a shot along it etc. You may wish to stop at different points along the route and suggest that the children take a photo.

   c. **Free walk**. Encourage the children to document a journey you take them on, taking the best photographs they can. This type of free photography activity is best left until the children have had several goes at activity a and b, and are more confident with using the cameras.

4. Once the digital photographs are uploaded there are lots of options on what to do with them depending upon the age and ability of your children:

   a. Invite the children to choose one or more of their own photos and write a caption to accompany it describing the subject, the type of shot and the result. The photos could be displayed on a wall, or the children could present them in a slideshow of their work in an assembly.

b. Ask the children to choose a favourite from their own photos, print it, make a circle and explain to the other children why they like it.

c. Use the photos to make a storyboard or story-map of the expedition either by arranging the photos and adding captions using word processing software or print out the photos and stick them down in the correct order on coloured sugar paper.

d. Use image manipulation software to alter the photos by changing colours, adding effects, including frames etc.

Variations

- Why not set up the activities in the context of a photography competition where the winners will receive a camera as a prize, or the winning photographs could be enlarged and framed for display somewhere in school.
- Try allowing the children to view some of their photographs enlarged on an interactive whiteboard.

Nature Sculptures

Nature Sculptures is an exciting project based upon the creations and installations of an artist from New Zealand called Chris Booth. Children will be amazed when they look at his work and inspired to go on and create their own.

Suitable for

KS1, KS2

Aims

- To use a range of materials to make sculptures.
- To investigate art from a variety of styles and genres.

Resources

- Interactive whiteboard and internet access (optional)
- Computers with internet access
- Digital camera (optional)
- Large collection of rocks, slate, pebbles, sticks, twigs and other nature objects
- Sticky pads, masking tape and string/fishing line, Blu-Tack/clay

What to do

1. Explain to the children that they are going to be studying the work of an artist named Chris Booth. Display his website on the interactive whiteboard: **www.chrisbooth.co.nz** Go to the 'Resume' section of the site and ask the children to pick out any facts that might tell them a little about the artist, or with younger children, tell them some information about the artist, e.g. born in New Zealand in 1948, worked with famous sculptors in the 1960s, has had exhibitions and created sculptures all over the world, has several books written about him and his artwork.

2. Go to the homepage and ask the children to choose a category to investigate from the following: slabs, boulders, earth blankets or columns. Look carefully at some of the images in each category and discuss the children's opinions and comment upon the materials used, the size of the sculptures, the techniques that may have been used to build them, colours and textures etc.

3. Explain to the children that they are going to be making their own nature sculpture in small groups using nature objects. (The sculptures will be on a much smaller scale than those of Chris Booth!) You can choose at this stage whether you want the children to collect their own materials or choose from a selection which you will provide. A combination of both works well.

4. Discuss some methods of joining/fixing objects in place using hidden sticky pads, tape, clay or string. Highlight the importance of balance in the sculptures, but stress that the children should not be afraid to experiment with unusual ideas and strange creative ways of arranging the objects.

5. Once the sculptures are complete, encourage the children to think of names for their creations and take some photographs of the results. Invite the class to present their work to the other children explaining what their sculpture is called and how it was constructed.

6. Depending upon where you decided to build the sculptures, they may need to be dismantled or they could be left temporarily for other children and parents to look at and enjoy.

Variations

- Rather than exploring the website to look at images of Chris Booth's art, you could look at a copy of the book: *Woven Stone – The Sculpture of Chris Booth*, Publisher: Random House NZ 2007 (Code: ISBN 978 1 86962 122 3). This would enable the whole session to be delivered outdoors. The book has many large pictures and lots of detail about the artist.
- You could turn the activity into a longer project by asking the children to design their nature sculpture on paper first and decide upon the best way to construct it before making.
- Extend the project by studying the work of other environmental artists – see **www.greenmuseum.org**.

Outdoor Chair

Designing an outdoor chair or bench can be an exciting challenge, especially when the project is set in a real life context. The children will design an outdoor chair for the school grounds based upon a real need. The best design/s can be built and installed, with help from the children.

Suitable for

KS1, KS2

Aims

- To design an object using drawings and labels.
- To generate ideas for products after thinking about who will use them and what they will be used for.

Resources

- Design sheets
- Pencils
- Rulers
- Real examples and photographs of outdoors chairs and benches
- Digital camera and printer (optional)

What to do

1. Explain to the children that they are going to be designing a new outdoor chair or bench for the school grounds, and the best design/s will actually be built and installed at school (optional).
2. Invite the children to decide upon appropriate locations for the new chair/bench to be positioned. At this point they could take photographs of their chosen spot to include in their design work later on.

3. Examine existing chairs and benches by looking at ones in or near to the school grounds. Discuss the features of some of the chairs/benches studied such as legs, seat, back, patterns, finish, materials used etc. Also discuss the children's opinions, likes and dislikes of the examples studied. As further research, the children could search for images on the internet using search terms such as: 'oak bench, garden seat, wooden outdoor chair'.

4. The children can then work individually or in pairs to design their own outdoor chair. The details of the design process will depend upon the age and ability of your class. A design sheet for younger children may just include a sketch and some labels. Here are some suggestions of things to include on a design sheet which older children could complete:

   a. **Brief** – a short description of the task

   b. **Notes** – details of research findings from examining existing chairs

   c. **Location** – a photograph and description of the spot where the new chair will be positioned

   d. **Purpose** – is the chair going to be used for storytelling/eating/looking at a view/sketching etc.

   e. **Drawings** – rough sketches of ideas for the new outdoor chair.

   f. **Final design** – detailed drawing with labels to explain key features, materials and construction thoughts

   g. **Views** – a bird's-eye and side elevation of the chair

   h. **Dimensions** – the size of the proposed bench including height, depth, width and seat height.

5. Once the children are happy with their design, you could invite them to share and pitch their designs to the rest of the class, and optionally, also to the headteacher or a governor.

6. The next stage is to choose the winning design/s. This could be done by the class teacher, headteacher or governors. Alternatively, ask the children to vote for their favourite design/s.

7. Once the winning design/s are chosen, then you have several options on how to get the chair/bench made:

   • Invite any parents who have carpentry skills to make the design.
   • Commission a local carpenter to make the design.

- Commission a specialist outdoor chairmaker such as
  www.oldforgewoodcraft.webs.com to make the design/s (email:
  oldforgewoodcraft@hotmail.co.uk). Here the children can have
  regular email/video-conferencing contact with the carpenter before,
  during and after; and they can be involved in the design and
  manufacturing process as much as possible.

8. Once the new chair/s are complete, they can be installed in their new
location and the children can evaluate the results.

Variations

- Why not take the design process further and ask older children to specify the
  kind of joints they would use to make the chair.
- You could allow the children to make scale models of their proposed design.
- How about having a plaque made which details the children's/designer's
  names and the date of construction?
- Invite the local press along to report on the project and take photos of the
  new chair/s being unveiled.

Seasons Pictures

Seasons Pictures are a useful way to help younger children recognise the effects which different seasons have upon the landscape/surrounding area/environment. For older children, Seasons Pictures can be a great way to experiment with different art tools and techniques or provide an excellent opportunity to develop photography skills.

Suitable for

KS1, KS2

Aims

- To combine and organise a variety of materials to make artefacts.
- To make observations about seasonal changes in the weather.

Resources

- Paper (good quality, thick art paper)
- Paints/crayons/felt tips/pastels/collage material/magazine cuttings/picture printouts from the internet
- Computers and art software (optional)
- Digital cameras (optional)

What to do

In its simplest form a Seasons Picture can be made as follows:

1. Divide a piece of paper into 4 sections, by folding in half and folding in half again.
2. Use a ruler and a black felt tip to mark out the 4 windows along the folds in the paper.

3. Label each window with one of the headings: *Spring, Summer, Autumn* and *Winter*.

4. Invite the children to create a picture which represents each season which includes the weather, the clothes you might wear, any festivals/celebrations that take place and activities that you might do in that particular season.

The following are variations on the simple activity:

- **Season by season** – complete one window of the picture in the actual season, rather than completing them all in one session.
- **Changing media** – complete each season window using a different medium, e.g. spring using paint/summer using collage/autumn using crayon/winter using pastel.
- **Computer art** – make a seasons picture using computer art software by mouse drawing, importing pictures or building up images with shapes and filling with colour. Combine the 4 completed images into one document, add labels and print.
- **Seasons photography** – make a seasons picture by printing and mounting, or pasting into a computer document, four photographic images which represent the seasons. They could be 4 photos taken of the same view at times during the different seasons. Alternatively, ask the children to take a photo in each season which represents the season well, e.g. a close-up shot of a daffodil to represent spring or a collection of colourful fallen leaves to represent autumn. (See Nature Photography on page 41 for some tips on improving photography skills.)

Variations

- Display the pictures with key vocabulary associated with the seasons to help with writing activities.
- Once a seasons window has been completed, write a poem or piece of descriptive writing to accompany each picture.

Shelter Making

Shelter Making is an activity which children always enjoy. Shelters can provide feelings of security and safety from the outside world; they are a great tool to stimulate creative play and can be made using almost any materials! Shelters can range from a playground structure made with boxes and a sheet, to a woodland hideaway made from logs, sticks and covered with foliage.

Suitable for

KS1, KS2

Aims

- To combine and organise a variety of materials to make artefacts.
- To listen to other people and play/work collaboratively.

Resources

- Scissors
- String/rope
- Parcel tape
- Pegs
- Objects to weigh corners down

Depending upon the type of shelter being made:

- Large cardboard boxes, bed-sheets
- Ground sheets/plastic sheeting, pegs
- Trees, long fallen sticks/branches, foliage

What to do

1. Shelters can be made using any of the materials listed above or anything which you have to hand, providing it results in a safe structure. They can be built on a playground, on a school field, against a wall, next to a fence or in woodland, with permission if needed.

2. When making a shelter try to make it as easy as possible by using any available existing features such as trees, branches or posts to act as a central pole. Use only fallen timber when working in woodland, unless you have permission and the appropriate equipment to safely cut branches and foliage.

3. Shelter building is an activity where it is useful to have plenty of adult helpers to support and supervise the groups. The normal safety procedures for working outdoors and handling nature objects should be followed by the children and helpers. Never allow children to enter a shelter until an adult has checked that it is safe to do so – this is a precaution mostly for working with heavy branches or poles.

4. You may wish to set the activity in the context of the shelter being built to provide cover from the sun, wind, cold or rain. You could set a time limit and award points at the end for the most successful shelters.

5. When the shelter is finished with, the children need to take them down carefully and make sure that there is no debris left behind.

   Here are some basic types of shelter which the children can make:

   a. **Lean-to Shelter**. This is a shelter made between 2 upright supports such as 2 trees, poles or tall box towers. A wedge shape is then made by attaching a long pole or rope line between the 2 uprights at approximately 1 metre up and then adding a cover such as a sheet, cardboard or foliage which runs back down to the ground on one side of the uprights. The cover can be secured to the ground with weights in the corners such as logs or rocks.

   b. **A-frame shelter**. This is a shelter in the shape of a triangular prism. It can be made by joining 2 poles together at either end on a 45 degree angle, then running a rope or a pole along the ridge between them and covering with branches/foliage or a sheet.

Alternatively, it can be made by making 2 large rectangular frames, then leaning them onto each other at a 45 degree angle and securing them with rope/string. The cover can be secured to the ground with weights. This type of shelter can also be built so that it slopes down along the ridge towards the back of the tent, thus making a doorway at one end.

c. **Tepee shelter**. This is a shelter which uses a large sheet or tarpaulin. A rope is attached to the top of a cone shape made using the sheet: hold the sheet landscape, hold a top corner and have another person wrap the top around until you can tie off the top with the rope. Leave a section of the rope trailing so that you can use this to tie the tepee top to a safe overhanging tree branch which has been inspected to make sure that it is in no danger of falling. The sheet can be secured to the ground using weights. Alternatively a central pole can be used to support the cover of the tepee.

* A useful tip for securing sheets or tarpaulins with a rope is to place a small item such as a rock or a stick on the underside, tie a loop in your rope/string, push the item through the loop with the sheet on top of it and tighten the knot.

d. **Tower shelter**. This is a simple shelter made by building secure towers from cardboard boxes and draping sheets or other materials to make a roof.

Variations

• Once built, shelters can be used as a base for other activities, games or play.
• Cardboard boxes and bed-sheets can be painted to make an extra-special shelter, or turn your tower shelter into a castle!

Sticky Pictures

Sticky Pictures is a simple activity which provides an opportunity for children to collect nature objects and make interesting designs. The finished pictures look great when displayed near a window or hung from the classroom ceiling.

Suitable for

KS1, KS2

Aim

- To combine and organise a variety of materials to make artefacts.

Resources

- Pieces of clear sticky-backed plastic
- Collection of nature objects
- String/ribbon
- Scissors
- Hole punch
- Sticky tape

What to do

1. Lead a short walk where the children can collect some nature objects. Encourage the children to choose objects that are relatively flat and thin, e.g. grass, leaves, petals.

2. Return to the classroom and peel off the backing sheets from the pieces of sticky-backed plastic, having secured the sheets to the tables using sticky tape in the corners. (You may need to do this for the children before collecting the nature objects as it can be a little fiddly.)

3. Explain to the children: 'Look at the nature objects you have collected and then place them onto your piece of sticky-backed plastic, thinking

about the way that they will look when hung up. You could try to make a pattern or arrange the objects in a shape that can be cut out. Remember not to have any bits sticking out over the edge of the plastic.'

4. Once the designs are complete, hand out a second piece of sticky-backed plastic (the same size as the first) and help the children peel off the backing and stick it down to sandwich their design.

5. Assist the children in cutting around their design to make a circle, make a hole at the top with a hole punch and thread some string through to hang the picture with.

Variations

- The children can create a nature collage individually, in pairs, in groups or as a whole class.
- You could link the activity to Maths by having groups make sticky pictures in regular 2D shapes, e.g. one group makes a circle, another group makes a square etc.

The Big Picture

The Big Picture is a collaborative painting activity on a large scale. The children use a bed-sheet as a backdrop to create their picture. Painting on a large vertical canvas is a great way to get everyone involved.

Suitable for

KS1, KS2

Aims

- To experiment with a variety of painting tools and techniques.
- To copy and enlarge images when painting.
- To work collaboratively.

Resources

- Painting aprons/shirts or old clothes to be worn
- Paint (ready mixed)
- Brushes and sponges
- Flat bed-sheet
- Drawing pins or hammer and tacks
- Multiple copies/printouts of a photograph
- Bowl of soapy water

What to do

1. Attach a flat bed-sheet securely to a fence/shed/wall using drawing pins or tacks. Be aware that paint may soak through onto the surface behind the sheet – you could mount some newspaper between the bed-sheet and the surface to limit this.

2. Hand out copies of a photograph. This could be a photo taken by one of the children in a previous lesson, (see Nature Photography on

page 41) a photo of the local area, a close up of some flowers etc. Make sure there is plenty of detail and interesting parts to the photo chosen, and ensure that it is of the same orientation as how the bed-sheet will be fixed, i.e. landscape or portrait.

3. Divide the photograph up into an appropriate number of sections which different children can work on. Depending upon the size of your class/group, you may want to have the children take turns at painting on the sheet.

4. Explain to the children: 'You are going to make a big picture on the sheet using paint. We are trying to enlarge the photograph, so concentrate on making your section look just like the original. I will tell you which part of the painting you are going to work on and remember that you will have to make that part bigger on the sheet. Try looking for key shapes and lines in your section which you can paint first. You can use brushes, sponges or your hands to paint with. There is a bowl of soapy water to clean your hands if you need to. You will need to work together as a group, so be helpful and patient.' (Use painting techniques appropriate to the age/ability of your class. Children painting the higher sections of the sheet may need something safe and stable to stand on.)

5. Once the painting is finished it can be evaluated by the children and displayed in school.

Variations

- The children can make a smaller Big Picture using half of a bed-sheet or old pillow cases, in pairs or in small groups.
- Why not link the activity with a study of an artist or an artistic style such as impressionism or pointillism?
- You may wish to teach children how to mix paint colours.
- You could ask the children to sketch out a rough outline of the key images/objects in the photo before painting begins, to help keep the picture to scale.
- If you are feeling 'brave' then you could attempt to recreate a painting in the abstract/expressionist style of Jackson Pollock with the children! It may be better to spread the sheet out on the floor in this instance and weight down the corners.

Wind Chime

Wind Chime making is a simple and enjoyable activity. You might need to ask parents for help in supplying some of the items to hang for the chimes.

Suitable for

KS1, KS2

Aim

- To combine and organise a variety of materials to make artefacts.

Resources

- Coat hangers/sticks/canes or hoops
- Scissors
- String/fishing line
- Collection of metal objects/objects which will make noise
- Pine cones/beads/heavy ring washers
- Screw eyes (optional)

What to do

1. Ask the children to choose 7 metal/noisy objects and something to hang them from, such as a coat hanger, stick, cane or a small hoop. The metal objects could include: old cutlery, buckles, hinges, buttons, washers etc.

2. Demonstrate how to measure and cut 7 pieces of string of the same length, and one piece of string which is longer. Ask the children to cut their string and tie an object onto one end of each of the shorter pieces.

3. Have the children lay the objects out on the table and try to arrange them under their hanger so that the weight across the wind chime will be balanced. Then the strings can be tied onto the hanger. The longer

piece of string needs to be attached to the bottom of the middle object in the row. A pine cone or some beads can be tied onto the bottom of the string which dangles below the middle to help catch the wind.

4. Hang the wind chimes outdoors with string in a suitable spot such as a tree/bush, hanging basket hook or climbing frame and listen to the results.

Variations

- Older children could use screw eyes to hang the objects from a wooden stick or dowel rod hanger. Pilot holes can be drilled with a hand drill to make screwing in easier.
- Why not try hanging other objects such as old CDs, lengths of hollow bamboo or shells.

Withy Sculptures

Withy Sculptures are a brilliant way of making 3D art with your class. Withies are flexible strong dried willow twigs which can be used to make many different kinds of sculpture. Take a look at the 'Phoenix' project for some ideas.

Suitable for

KS1, KS2

Aims

- To assemble, combine and join components thinking about how the working characteristics of materials affect the ways they are used.
- To create interesting 3D objects.

Resources

To make a 'Phoenix':
- Withies (pre-soaked in water for 24 hours)
- Masking tape
- Tissue paper
- Foil paper
- PVA glue and spreaders
- 1 strong bamboo garden cane per sculpture

What to do

1. Withies are extremely versatile to work with. You can create all kinds of objects such as animals, shapes, people or structures. The children should ideally work in small groups when using withies.

2. Before starting a project with the children you may wish to show them the work of some other willow sculptors such as Serena de la Hey (www.serenadelahey.com) who is best known for 'Willow Man' – a

12 metre high willow figure which can be seen alongside the M5 near Bridgwater, Somerset.

3. Here is an art project which demonstrates some of the basic principles of how to use withies. 'Phoenix' was led by Clare Summerson (**www.casummerson.freeuk.com**). Children from both Key Stages 1 & 2 made the phoenix sculptures in groups of 5.

Instructions for making a withy sculpture:

a. Soak the withy lengths in water for 24 hours before you plan to use them.

b. Bend the withy lengths to make 2D shapes (e.g. circles or leaf shapes) and secure the ends with masking tape. Fasten these shapes together with more masking tape to form 3D objects (e.g. a body, wings or head).

c. Once you have combined these parts together they can be mounted onto a strong bamboo cane.

d. Cover the whole structure with tissue paper which has been pasted all over with watered down PVA glue.

e. Add decoration by sticking on tissue or foil paper.

Variations

- Withy sculptures can be built for internal or external use. External sculptures usually consist of just the willow frame rather than decorating them. For outdoor sculptures use garden twine or string to secure the withies rather than masking tape. Withies can be treated with linseed oil to prolong their life outdoors. You could also grow climbing plants up the structures.
- Why not demonstrate the properties of withies, then ask the children to design a sculpture in small groups to be built in stages over several lessons.
- You could invite the children to design a sculpture for a specific location in the school grounds or school building.

Chapter 3
English

Drama Garden

Drama Garden is a collection of drama session ideas which will help children to explore nature through improvisation and mime. They are exciting and useful activities which can be used as a stimulus for creative writing as well as for learning about nature.

Suitable for

KS1, KS2

Aims

- To use language and actions to explore and convey situations.
- To create and sustain dramatic roles.
- To explore plant and animal behaviour using dramatic techniques.

Resources

- Musical instruments (optional)
- CD player and appropriate music (optional)
- Digital camera (optional)
- Video camera (optional)

What to do

The following are a selection of outdoor drama ideas which could be used as the main activity in separate lessons, or delivered together as shorter workshops in one session.

1. Growing – the children pretend to be plants or trees which begin life as a seed, push through the soil, grow into a seedling and then grow up into a full plant or tree. One or more children could act as a gardener and move around the other children 'watering' and 'nurturing' the seedlings, as each seedling receives more water it is able to grow larger. A child could represent the sun coming in and out

and the plants react accordingly. The children could work in small groups to represent one tree.

2. **Moving** – the children pretend to be trees in a forest anchored into the ground by their roots. They then react dramatically to the changing weather conditions initiated by you or a child, such as: rain, a light breeze, thunder storm, strong wind, a hurricane, sunshine etc. Musical instruments could be used to signal the different weather conditions, i.e. rain stick for light rain, crashing cymbals for a storm, rolling drums and recorders for strong wind.

3. **Sensory garden** – the children explore an imagined outdoor environment such as a rainforest or a river bed. They can either act as humans exploring in the environment using their senses, or become small animals/creatures experiencing the environment. The children could discuss or write about their journey afterwards.

4. **Garden pictures** – the children work in groups to create scenes from a given nature environment (e.g. an English woodland or Brazilian rainforest), some children represent particular plants and trees, whilst others act as animals moving around. Freeze and unfreeze the moving pictures to allow yourself or other children to examine the scene and suggest what they think the actors are representing.

5. **Big scenes** – the children work as a class to act out one large scene. Have one or two children (or yourself) act as directors who instruct the others on who or what they should be. Some children will be animals moving around the scene whilst others are being the trees and plants. Try to tell the story of a day and a night in that environment. Use music to help give time cues and to change the scene from day into night. You could video-record the performance and play it back to the children.

Variations

- You could play relevant music through a CD player which helps the children sustain their roles in the nature scenarios.
- Try taking digital photographs which the children can look at and write about what they were doing in a particular drama activity.

Nature Guide Book

> Nature Guide Book is a writing-based project which sees the children produce a useful reference guide to help other children learn about the animal and plant life in a chosen area.

Suitable for

KS1, KS2

Aims

- To write using language and a style that are appropriate to the reader.
- To use the features of layout, presentation and organisation correctly.
- To learn about different plants and animals found in a local environment.

Resources

- Clipboards, paper and pencils/pens
- Field guides – flowers/animals/insects etc.
- Digital cameras (optional)
- Computers (optional)

What to do

1. Explain to the children that they are going to be writing a Nature Guide Book for your chosen area. This could be the school nature area, a beach, the school field, local woodland, a field, a stream/river etc. The guide book will be for other children in school to take with them when they explore the chosen area. It will help to describe the area and its inhabitants.

2. Decide upon the format of the Nature Guide Book. Are you going to make one book as a whole class with partners working on different sections; or will you have the children making separate nature guide books in small groups or pairs?

3. Here are some suggestions for the contents of a Nature Guide Book:

- Map of the area
- Directions to the area
- Nature walk route
- Animals
- Insects
- Birds
- Plants
- Trees
- How to act
- Safety.

4. Once the children understand which part of the guide book they will be responsible for writing, they can begin to do their research. The research will usually involve a visit to the chosen location to study, make notes, take photographs and identify species.

5. After the research stage, the children will write up their findings, following appropriate non-fiction writing conventions. You could supply the children with writing frames or give some example formats for the book pages. Discuss the importance of pictures, labels and the style of language needed. The Nature Guide Book can be hand-written, word-processed or a combination of both. As their contribution to the book, younger children might label and colour a picture of one of the birds found in the area; older children might draw the bird, label its body parts, describe its appearance and write 3 facts which they have learned about it.

6. Once the guide books are complete then they can be given to other children to use on a visit to the chosen area, who will then report back to the authors about their experience.

Variations

- The children could create a website or PowerPoint presentation to accompany the guide book.
- Why not make copies of the guide books and offer them to members of the local community.

Outdoor Poetry

Outdoor Poetry is a creative session where the children take inspiration from their surroundings. This is a great way to make children focus on some of the smaller details in nature by concentrating on their senses.

Suitable for

KS1, KS2

Aims

- To write poetry based on a firsthand experience.
- To use words to explore an experience.
- To explore using the senses of sight, hearing, smell, touch and taste.

Resources

- Clipboards, paper and pencils
- Tape/digital audio-recorder (optional)
- Digital camera (optional)

What to do

1. Lead the children to an outdoor location. This can be anywhere that there will be things to explore using the senses e.g. a beach, woodland, the school field/playground etc.

2. Have the children sit down in a circle and explain that they are going to be using their senses to explore the environment which surrounds them and that they will need to use good adjectives to describe what they see, hear, smell, touch and taste.

3. Ask the children to divide their paper up into 5 sections (if you intend to cover all 5 senses) and label each one with a different sense. (This could be done before leaving the classroom or printed onto a worksheet to save time.)

4. Go through the senses, one at a time with the children, allowing them to experience and absorb their surroundings e.g. 'Close your eyes and listen to all of the sounds which you can hear, in one minute I will tell you to open your eyes and start to write down some details of what you heard remembering to use good describing words.' Encourage the children to be silent during each sensory exploration, and then share their thoughts, ideas and descriptions after each one has been completed. Tasting will only be appropriate in certain situations, you could purchase or grow some strawberries for the children to taste and describe if you are writing poetry outside on a summer's day. If you plan to eat any wild fruit such as blackberries, then ensure they are washed, and take the time to explain the dangers of eating berries or any wild food, i.e. only eat the ones which you know are edible, use a guide book if necessary to help identify it, wash the food if need be and if you are in any doubt – don't eat it because it could be poisonous.

5. Once the children have completed the sensory exploration, you can model how to turn some of their descriptive phrases into a poem. This can be done in many ways depending upon the age and ability of your class. You could ask them to write an acrostic, calligram, *haiku* or free verse.

6. Allow the children to read aloud their poems whilst still in the environment they are describing.

7. Invite the children to make evaluative comments on things which they liked about the others' poems.

Variations

- You could take a photograph of the environment being described to display next to the children's work back at school.
- Why not use a tape/digital audio-recorder to capture the sounds being heard. This will be useful if you need to return to the classroom to write the poems.
- Share some poems with the children which have been written by famous poets such as Alice Oswald or Ted Hughes, choose poems which describe a similar environment to the one you are going to be studying.

Outdoor Storytime

> Outdoor Storytime is a collection of reading and speaking/listening activities. Listening to a story being told outdoors is a brilliant experience which can have a very different feel from hearing a story indoors.

Suitable for

KS1, KS2

Aims

- To read aloud with confidence.
- To gain and maintain the interest and response of an audience.
- To understand how to be a good listener.
- To use imagination to create mental pictures derived from a story.

Resources

- Storybooks relevant to ability and topic
- Storyteller chair
- Mini-whiteboard and pen

What to do

The following are a collection of storytelling activities and discussions which can be used outdoors. Where possible the storyteller should be in a higher position than the audience, either standing or seated on a storyteller chair. (Why not design and make a storyteller chair for your own outdoor classroom – see page 46, Outdoor Chair.)

1. **Good storytelling** – a discussion with the children on what makes a good storyteller. You could begin by reading in a very boring, monotonous, stilted fashion and ask the children what needs to be improved in your reading to make you into a good storyteller. Make a list

of what you decide are the important areas on a mini-whiteboard. Some aspects of storytelling which could be discussed are: eye contact with the audience; facial expression; gesturing with the body; using the voice effectively; the pace of your speaking; and good descriptive language (if storytelling without a book).

2. **Good listening** – a discussion with the children on what makes a good listener. Why not begin by asking a child to read aloud to you and you can demonstrate what a bad listener would do. Ask the children to share their suggestions for improving your listening skills. Write down the important skills on a mini-whiteboard. The list of skills might include: sitting still and quietly; responding with laughter, gestures, nodding, eye contact, facial expression; and using imagination to create mental pictures.

3. **Outdoor reading** – the children read to each other in pairs or small groups using school reading books. The groups can be mixed or similar ability. Encourage the children to focus on developing an aspect of their reading/storytelling such as pausing to build tension or using different voices for characters.

4. **Storytelling** – the children tell stories to each other in pairs or small groups from memory rather than by reading aloud from a book. This type of storytelling requires plenty of modelling, lots of practice and a good understanding of the skills outlined in activities 1 and 2. Here are some tips to improve storytelling without a book:

   a. First model how to tell stories without the book yourself, and ask the children to identify things which made you a good storyteller.

   b. Focus on a well known traditional/fairytale such as 'Red Riding Hood' or 'Goldilocks and the Three Bears' for the children's first attempt. Begin by allowing the children to read the story from a book in a version appropriate to their reading ability, then you could retell the story yourself without using the book as an example, finally allow the children to retell without a book.

   c. Break the story down into smaller chunks by having the children work in groups of three and split a story into its beginning, middle and end. Each child retells one section of the story and the other children help if they find any parts difficult. Practise several times and then the groups could share their story with the rest of the class.

   d. Encourage the children to draw a series of pictures/sketches which represent the key events in a story. This can help children visualise and remember the plot. The pictures could be placed close by as a quick prompting tool for the storyteller to glance at. (This technique was suggested by Will Coleman, an excellent storyteller who has written some fantastic children's books which can be used to develop storytelling without the book, see: **www.bravetales.co.uk**.)

   e. More able children could write their own stories which they will then learn, practise and finally perform/retell for others.

5. **Sound effects** – get the children to use musical instruments, body percussion or nature objects to create sound effects in appropriate places in a story as it is read aloud. It may take several attempts at reading the story for the children to identify places for sound effects, to find the best way of making them and to practise performing them. On a final retelling of the story the children can play the sound effects in the correct places seamlessly.

6. **Local stories** – when outside, tell the children stories about the local area including local people, historical events or improvised tales based on the local environment. A special significance and a whole new level of involvement can be reached by the children if a story takes place on or near the location where they are sat, or if the story is about things which they can see, hear and touch. (Try inviting a local storyteller or local historian to visit your outdoor classroom – see the companion website for details of storytellers in your region.)

Post It

> Post It is an activity which teaches children about letter writing and helps towards establishing a culture of writing letters to friends. Try coupling this activity with another activity such as 'Farm Visit' to give some ideas for the contents of the children's letters.

Suitable for

KS1, KS2

Aims

- To write a letter to a classmate using language and a style that are appropriate to the reader.
- To understand how written English varies in the degrees of formality.

Resources

- Clipboards, paper and pencils/pens
- Envelopes
- Postbox
- Name cards in a hat

What to do

1. Have the children sit outside in a circle. Give every child a blank name card to write their full name on. Pass a hat or box around the circle and collect all the name cards.

2. Pass the hat back around the circle and each child needs to take out a name from the hat and keep it a secret, unless they pick out their own name, in which case they should swap it for another!

3. Explain that the children are going to write a letter to the person whose name was on the card they chose. Teach/remind the children

about the appropriate conventions for writing a letter to a friend and how this will differ from writing a formal letter. The amount and level of input you give will depend upon the age and ability of the children. You could give some suggestions about the kinds of things the children could include e.g. some questions for the reader, some interesting things about themselves, their likes and dislikes, the favourite thing about a recent trip etc. You could read an example letter which you have written to a friend.

4. Hand out clipboards and paper, and allow the children to find a space outdoors to work in to write their letter. You may wish to provide a writing frame for some children to help structure their letter.

5. Once the children have finished writing their letter, have them bring it to you to be checked before you issue them with an envelope. They should then write the recipient's name and the school address on the envelope and post it into a postbox. (The postbox could be one which you make with the children to be sited permanently outside, or one which has been purchased for that purpose. By having a postbox outside you can begin to encourage a culture of friends writing to one another.)

6. Have a postmaster empty the postbox, and a postwoman or postman deliver the letters to the children. These jobs could be made into regular positions/monitors with the responsibility of delivering the mail from the school postbox on a weekly basis.

Variations

- Why not invite the children to write a reply to their letter in a following lesson.
- You could join with another school and have the children write letters and replies to each other.
- Younger children could draw and label a picture of the things they like and dislike to form the main body of their letter.

Chapter 4
Humanities

Anemometer

An Anemometer is a device which measures how fast the wind is blowing. This is a making activity where the children can build their own anemometer. The finished device can then be used to record information about the wind speed.

Suitable for

KS1, KS2

Aims

- To observe, record and use fieldwork skills.
- To identify and describe the weather and seasonal changes.
- To use a range of materials to make weather instruments.

Resources

- 4 small paper cups
- Strong drawing pin
- Coloured sticky dots or a marker pen
- 2 long strong plastic drinking straws
- Stapler
- New pencil with a rubber on the end
- Sticky tape
- Scissors
- Stopwatch

What to do

Explain to the children that they are going to be making an anemometer. You could explain what an anemometer does and ask them to design their own, or supply them with the following design:

1. Lie one of the drinking straws across the other to make a cross shape and wrap sticky tape around the middle to secure them.

2. Staple one paper cup to all four ends of the straws so that they can catch the wind and spin around. The cups must face in the same direction. The cups can be trimmed down to make them lighter when hanging under the straws if necessary.

3. Mark one of the cups with a marker pen or sticky dots to make counting the revolutions easier late on.

4. Push the drawing pin through the exact centre of the straw cross and then into the centre of the rubber on the end of the pencil. Make sure that the cups spin freely in the wind.

5. Push the pencil into the grass or earth in an open location. (Alternatively fill an empty drinks bottle with gravel, push the pencil in and tape up the top.)

6. Measure the wind speed by counting the number of times that the coloured cup spins around in a set time (1 or 2 minutes). Use a stopwatch to time the event and record the number of revolutions on a chart. (The results will not give you an exact reading of the wind speed, but will give you a relative indication of how fast the wind is blowing.)

Variations

- The children could make one anemometer each, take them home and record the wind speed over a set period as homework.
- Why not make some other weather instruments and complete a weather report or a weather project. (See page 95.)
- Challenge more able children to find a way of calibrating their anemometer so that it can be used to give a reading in mph.
- Try measuring the wind speed at different times of the day and in different locations.

Farm Visit

> A Farm Visit can be an excellent learning opportunity for children. Many farms are happy to accommodate school parties and the children will enjoy meeting and working with the people and animals.

Suitable for

KS1, KS2

Aims

- To meet and talk with people to learn about them and their lifestyle.
- To identify how and why places change.
- To recognise how and why people may seek to manage environments sustainably.

Resources

Resources will vary according to each individual farm visit, but here are some suggestions for commonly required items:

- First aid kit including inhalers (check beforehand for any children with animal allergies)
- Drinks and food
- Waterproofs
- Wellies/appropriate footwear
- Group lists
- Paper/nature log books (see page 12.)

What to do

Organising a farm visit can provide a wealth of learning opportunities for children. What follows are some suggestions for activities children can do when visiting a working farm. Careful preparation for a farm visit is essential, a preliminary visit should be undertaken and risk assessments completed with help from the farming staff. There are several organisations which can be of assistance in finding farms to visit. Visit the Farming and Countryside Education (FACE) website for more help and advice – www.face-online.org.uk. Alternatively, approach a local farm yourself.

Activity ideas:

- **Farm tour** – a guided exploration of the farm stopping at places of interest to talk with the farmer.
- **Observational drawing** – animals, vehicles, landscapes, buildings.
- **Photography** – (see page 41).
- **Animal study** – learn about the animals on farms and their uses.
- **Crop study** – learn about the crops grown on farms and their uses.
- **Animal welfare** – discuss animal welfare with the farmer and the steps the farm takes.
- **Interview** – the children prepare interview questions to pose to the farmer or farm staff and take notes of the answers.
- **Farm jobs** – can the children assist with any jobs on the farm such as feeding the animals?
- **History** – investigate how farming has changed with the advance of modern technology.
- **Difficulties** – discover the difficulties which farms face in a modern society.
- **Sustainability** – find out what the farm does to ensure that its practices are sustainable.
- **Quiz** – ask questions at the end of the visit with prizes for correct answers.
- **Treasure trail** – before a tour of the farm begins, position tokens or toy animals in different places on the route. Whenever a child finds a token, ask the class a question based on the tour so far, if it is answered correctly then a prize is awarded.

Variations

- If you have lots of outdoor space on your school grounds you could consider the option of keeping animals yourself. There are many support networks to help set this up.

- Visit the same farm at different times of the year to learn about the varying jobs that take place.
- When the children return to school, teach cross-curricular linked lessons based on their farm visit, e.g. Maths – calculating quantities of feed required for the animals; Art – turn the sketches drawn on the visit into watercolour paintings; ICT – prepare PowerPoint presentations using photographs taken on the visit.

Making Tracks

Making Tracks is a game where children make tracks and trails for others to follow. Following symbols and signs made from nature objects is great fun, especially if there is a prize at the end!

Suitable for

KS1, KS2

Aims

- To use fieldwork skills – to make maps and plans.
- To learn symbols and follow directions.
- To work collaboratively.

Resources

- Collection of nature objects
- String
- Prizes/rewards

What to do

Making Tracks can be done in the school grounds, in a local outdoor space or woodland. There are a number of ways to organise a Making Tracks game:

Making Tracks with nature objects –

1. The teacher or an adult helper secretly makes a track for the children to follow in small groups. The children follow the clues (see below for clue ideas) on the track to find their way to a prize.

2. A small group of children make a track with clues for the other groups to follow. The group making the track can be rotated each time the game is played.

Making Tracks on maps –

3. The teacher creates a track by marking a route onto a simple drawn map of the school grounds. Use symbols and arrows to lead groups of children to the prize.

4. Groups of children use a paper copy of the simple map of the school grounds to create a track for other groups to follow. Encourage the groups to walk/follow the trail themselves before allowing others to use it.

You can give the children some ideas on how to make symbols using nature objects, or encourage them to develop their own:

- Use twigs arranged into an arrow shape to show which direction to travel.
- Use stones to make letters such as N S E W or L R to show which direction to travel.
- Use twigs to make a no entry sign in places where the track does not go.
- Make a code key which the children following the trail could carry with them, or make them try to remember it. A code key explains what shapes made with twigs on the track stand for, e.g. a triangle on the path = turn right, a square on the path = turn left, a cross on the path = the end of the track etc.

Variations

- Have the children create their own simple plan maps of the school grounds by working outdoors in pairs and plotting the key buildings and notable features such as large trees, fences, playgrounds, car parks and gates.
- Try hanging clues from tree branches using string. These could be simple picture maps which show the direction to the next clue.
- You could use chalk to create temporary signs and symbols on the playground.

Nature Treasure Hunt

A Nature Treasure Hunt is a brilliant way to keep children busy on a nature walk or a fun activity to complete in its own right. The children have a list of items which they need to find.

Suitable for

KS1, KS2

Aims

- To investigate objects and materials using their senses.
- To look closely and find out about nature objects.

Resources

- Collection bags
- Nature Treasure Hunt lists
- Pencils
- Nature log books (optional)
- Magnifying glasses (optional)

What to do

1. Lead a walk/trip to an area rich in nature objects, or use the school grounds if appropriate.

2. The children work in groups of 2 or 3. Each group needs a Nature Treasure Hunt list, a collection bag and a pencil.

3. Explain to the children that they need to find as many of the objects from the list as they can. You may wish to read through the list with the children before they set off.

4. Make sure that the children are fully aware of the boundaries of the area in which they are allowed to search, discuss what it is safe/responsible to pick up and what to avoid. Make sure you have adequate adult supervision when allowing children to explore in this way.

5. Once the children have collected the objects from the list, they could lay them out on the ground and choose some to sketch in their nature log books, show and talk about their 'beautiful' nature object in an outdoor circle time session or have an adult count up how many objects the group found from the list.

Here are some suggestions for your Nature Treasure Hunt list:

Something beautiful	A seed	A large leaf
A small leaf	Something round	Something soft
25 of something	A berry	A daisy
Something shiny	A forked stick	Something with tiny
Something patterned	Something white	details
An oak leaf		

Variation

- Give the children a list or pictures of things to look out for on a walk such as: a bird's nest, a stone wall, a stile, a sheep, a ladybird.

Orienteering

Orienteering is an enjoyable and practical way to develop key Geography skills whilst improving fitness! It can be done on the school playground, field or out in the local environment with the appropriate supervision.

Suitable for

KS1, KS2

Aims

- To use maps and plans including contents, keys and grids.
- To use appropriate geographical vocabulary.

Resources

- Large-scale maps of the orienteering area
- Go to www.britishorienteering.org.uk for comprehensive advice and a range of local contacts who will help you to organise events
- Compasses/punches/labels/stakes/pencils (depending upon how you organise your orienteering course)

What to do

1. The orienteering course which you create should be tailored to the age and ability of your children. Contact your local development officer through www.britishorienteering.org.uk for advice on this, or to find out if there are any existing orienteering courses in your local area.

2. An orienteering course can be created in its simplest form by: drawing a large-scale map of the school environment which includes key fixed features; creating a set of letter cards (these should make a word/phrase when written in the correct order) which need to be attached at various locations in the school environment; and labelling

the map with numbers which correspond to the location of the letter cards. Photocopy the map and leave a space for the children to write down the letters which they find at the numbered points on the map.

3. Explain to the children: 'You are going to work in pairs to find out the secret word/phrase hidden on the orienteering course. You will need to use the map to find your way to all of the different numbered points, at each number you will find a letter. Write down the letters on your map and arrange them correctly to make the secret word/phrase.'

4. You should start the pairs off at different numbers or at timed intervals to avoid congestion and to avoid pairs following each other rather than following the map.

Variations

- Once the children are familiar with this simple technique then you could introduce compasses and directions to the orienteering course.
- Why not turn the activity into a competition, where the fastest pairs receive a prize.

Rain Gauge

A Rain Gauge measures how much rain has fallen in a set location. This is a simple making activity where the children can make their own Rain Gauge. The finished device can be used to record the daily rainfall.

Suitable for

KS1, KS2

Aims

- To observe, record and use fieldwork skills.
- To identify and describe the weather and seasonal changes.
- To use a range of materials to make weather instruments.

Resources

- Scissors
- Clear sticky tape
- Plastic ruler
- 2L plastic drinks bottle
- Paper
- Pencil

What to do

Explain to the children that they are going to be making a rain gauge. You could discuss what a rain gauge does and ask them to design their own to begin with, or supply them with the following design:

1. Measure down 15cm from the top of the drinks bottle and mark a line around the label. Cut carefully around the line to leave you with a top and bottom. (You may need to cut the bottles depending on the age and ability of your children.)

2. Remove the lid from the bottle cap and place the neck upside down inside the bottom section of the bottle.

3. Use clear sticky tape to attach a plastic ruler to the outside of the rain gauge. Make sure the cm scale begins at the base of the bottle.

4. Find a safe piece of open ground to position the rain gauge. You could use some rocks or bricks to keep the gauge upright in windy weather, alternatively, bury the gauge partially in soil or challenge the children to develop some kind of stand/support which keeps their rain gauge stable.

5. Measure the rainfall daily by looking at the ruler to see how far the gauge has been filled, then empty the rainwater and replace the gauge ready for the next day.

Variations

- The children could make one rain gauge each, take them home and record the rainfall over a set period as homework.
- Why not make some other weather instruments and complete a weather report or a weather project. (See page 95.)

Weather Report

Weather Report is a collection of ideas based on the theme of the weather. Children will enjoy measuring with instruments as well as recording and interpreting the results.

Suitable for

KS1, KS2

Aims

- To observe, record and use fieldwork skills.
- To identify and describe the weather and seasonal changes.
- To use a range of materials to make weather instruments.

Resources

- Clipboards
- Pencils
- Recording grids (paper- or computer-based)
- Thermometer
- Anemometer
- Wind vane
- Rain gauge

What to do

1. **Forecast.** Watch some examples of weather forecasts from television or the internet. Discuss the features of a weather forecast, e.g: predicting the forthcoming weather; reporting on past weather; air temperatures; wind speed and direction; atmospheric conditions; rainfall etc. Invite the children to make their own weather forecast to be performed to the class or recorded using a video camera.

2. **Weather station**. Collect data about the weather over a set period using a thermometer, anemometer, wind vane and a rain gauge (see pages 82, 93 and 97 for instructions on how to make these). Analyse and interpret the results to create statements about the weather in that set period. You could allow children to collect data themselves at home and then compare the results with those of their classmates.

3. **Extreme weather**. Ask groups of children to study different aspects of extreme weather, e.g. tsunami, hurricane, thunder storm etc. Each group prepares a display, PowerPoint presentation, a talk or an information book page on their weather topic.

Variation

- You could set up a weather area in the classroom by displaying a map (local or national) and supplying weather symbols with Blu-Tack on the back to stick onto the map. The children can then act out their own weather reports.

Wind Vane

A Wind Vane is a device which shows in which direction the wind is blowing. This is a making activity where the children can build their own Wind Vane. The finished device can then be used to record information about the direction the wind is travelling from.

Suitable for

KS1, KS2

Aims

- To observe, record and use fieldwork skills.
- To identify and describe the weather and seasonal changes.
- To use a range of materials to make weather instruments.

Resources

- Corriflute 2 A4 sheets (or corrugated card and sticky-backed plastic)
- Pen lid (or a long thin tube such as a Smarties tube)
- Sticky tape
- Gravel or sand
- Funnel
- 2L plastic drinks bottle
- Thin wooden dowel rod (2 pieces × 40cm long)
- Blu-Tack
- Plastic magnetic letters N, E, S, W (or card labels)

What to do

Explain to the children that they are going to be making a wind vane. You could explain what a wind vane does and ask them to design their own, or supply them with the following design:

1. Cut out 2 identical arrow shapes from the corriflute card. Place them on either side of the pen top/Smarties tube and use sticky tape to fix them both together with the pen top/Smarties tube sandwiched between them.

2. Cut one of the dowel rods into 4 smaller pieces of equal length (10cm). Carefully make holes halfway down the bottle and push the ends of the dowel rods through the holes leaving most of the rod sticking out of the bottle. Use a small piece of tape around each hole to secure the rod. Make sure that the 4 rods are positioned at 90 degree angles to each other. Attach the plastic letters to the 4 ends of the rods to mark out the compass points North, East, South and West.

3. Use the funnel to fill the bottle two-thirds full with sand or gravel and check that the compass point markers are still in the correct position.

4. Place the long dowel rod in the bottle, pushing it down securely into the sand/gravel. Put some Blu-Tack in the neck of the bottle around the dowel rod to help keep it in a central position. Wrap some sticky tape around this to add extra stability.

5. Place the pen top/Smarties tube onto the dowel rod and check that the arrows spin freely in the wind.

6. Position the wind vane in open ground and use a compass to align North on the wind vane with magnetic north.

7. Measure and record the wind direction at regular intervals.

Variations

- The children could make one wind vane each, take them home and record the wind direction over a set period as homework.
- Why not make some other weather instruments and complete a weather report or a weather project. (See page 95.)

Woodland Layers

Woodland Layers is an activity where the children learn about trees from the ground upwards. They will explore the purpose, construction and animals found in the different layers of woodland.

Suitable for

KS1, KS2

Aims

- To identify and understand the different layers of woodland.
- To observe and identify features in the natural world.

Resources

- Digital camera (optional)
- Nature log books/paper
- Pencils

What to do

1. Lead a visit to an area of woodland with well established trees.
2. Begin at ground level and discuss each layer as listed below. Have the children draw a simple sketch of each layer and label its functions. They could draw some of the creatures you might find there too.

   a. **Soil layer** – is the base of the forest, supporting and providing moisture and nutrients to plant and tree roots. It is made up of decomposed plant matter and inorganic material, such as rocks, minerals and clay.

   b. **Litter layer** – is the organic debris on the floor of the forest, it is made up of decaying plant matter and fungi. Bacteria, insects and worms in the litter help to break down the plant matter.

c. **Field layer** – is the first layer of growth above the litter and soil. It can be up to 2 metres high. It can consist of low herbaceous plants, mosses, ferns, wildflowers and grasses. It is a habitat for insects, mammals, reptiles and amphibians.

d. **Understorey** – is made up of vines, mosses, shrubs, bushes and tree seedlings reaching up towards the canopy; it is a habitat for birds and insects.

e. **Canopy** – is the highest layer of the forest. It is formed by the branches/crowns of mature trees that shade and protect the lower layers. The canopy provides a habitat for insects, birds and small mammals.

Variation

- Woodland Layers makes an excellent interactive display back in the classroom. The children can help to make the trees and write labels which explain the different woodland layers and functions.

Chapter 5
Maths

Outdoor Patterns

> Outdoor Patterns is a practical and creative Maths activity which younger children will enjoy. They will need to find, identify and record patterns they find.

Suitable for

KS1

Aim

- To recognise simple patterns and make predictions about them.

Resources

- Wax crayons
- Drawing paper
- Coloured marker cones (optional)
- Magnifying glasses (optional)
- Digital camera (optional)

What to do

1. Have the children sit in a circle outdoors. Discuss what is meant by the word 'pattern' (an arrangement of repeated parts, colours or shapes). Ask if any of the children have patterns on their clothing, shoes or socks. Explain that patterns can be found in many places outdoors – some are made by nature and some are man-made.

2. Challenge the children to spot a pattern from where they are seated in the circle – e.g. a pattern found on a picket fence, the bricks in a wall etc. Explain that sometimes we need to look very closely to see the patterns that are made by nature. (You could demonstrate how to use a magnifying glass.)

3. Allow the children to explore the outdoor space available with clearly set boundaries, if necessary, and as much adult supervision as is required. They will need to find and record as many patterns as they can. The children could record the patterns by making rubbings with wax crayons, drawing pictures, leaving a coloured marker cone near the pattern and returning with the other children on a tour of the cones later on.

4. Return to the outdoor circle or classroom and share some of the interesting patterns found.

Variations

- Use a digital camera to capture photographs of the patterns identified by the children. Have the children make large paintings of these and create a display in the classroom. The display could challenge the children to find the patterns and predict what will happen next in the sequence.
- Use the nature/outdoor theme to continue work on patterns with numbers, e.g. what if the number of petals on a daisy decreasing in steps of 1 as a bird pulls them off 25, 24, 23, 22 ...

Buried Treasure

Buried Treasure is an enjoyable game which teaches children about direction, movement and compass points. The children will need to give clear and precise instructions if they are to successfully navigate their way to the treasure.

Suitable for

KS1, KS2

Aims

- To recognise and use the four compass points: N, S, E, W.
- To understand direction.
- To give clear and accurate instructions.

Resources

- North, south, east, west cards
- Treasure (e.g. stickers/sweets or healthy snacks/tokens for golden time/stationery prizes)
- Treasure map (basic plan maps of the site with Xs marked in a number of locations to show where the treasure is hidden)

What to do

1. Before the outdoor session begins, bury/place some treasure in a few well hidden spots around the site.
2. When the session begins, have the children sit facing in the same direction. Display four compass point cards on stakes or chairs in the corresponding directions around where the children will sit: North (N), South (S), East (E) and West (W).
3. Explain to the children: 'I have buried some treasure somewhere in this area. One child will be the treasure hunter, and the other children will

be the navigators. The navigators will take turns to shout one instruction at a time to the treasure hunter. The instructions can only include a compass point and a number of steps e.g. 'move 5 steps north' or 'move 4 steps east.' The navigator will know where to direct the treasure hunter because there will be a treasure map being handed around the group. The navigator has 30 seconds to look at the map, decide on an instruction and shout it out, the map is then passed to the next navigator until the hunter has found a piece of treasure.'

4. Once a piece of treasure is found, a new treasure hunter can be chosen. This could be the last navigator to give an instruction before the hunter found the treasure, or simply done in register order.

Variations

- Once the children are confident with the game and know the direction of the compass points, the compass point cards can be taken down.
- You could choose one child to be the navigator and give all of the instructions to the treasure hunter.
- The game can be extended by limiting the number of instructions which the navigators are allowed to give to the treasure hunter. The number of instructions used can be recorded in a tally chart. This encourages the children to find the shortest route to the treasure. If the treasure hunter doesn't reach the treasure once all of the instructions are used up, then one piece of treasure belongs to the teacher.
- The number of compass points used can be increased to 8, i.e. N, NE, E, SE, S, SW, W and NW.

Compass Jumping

Compass Jumping is an enjoyable and active game which can be used to teach children about direction, right angles and compass points.

Suitable for

KS1, KS2

Aims

- To recognise the four compass points: N, S, E, W.
- To recognise right angles.
- To develop an understanding of clockwise and anti-clockwise direction.

Resources

- Compass (optional)
- North, south, east, west cards (optional)

What to do

1. Have the children stand outside in a space, all facing in the same direction.
2. Explain to the children: 'We are going to be jumping to face a compass point of North (N), South (S), East (E) or West (W). If we face the school, we are facing North. If we turn and face in the opposite direction, we will be facing South. From facing North, if we turn 1 right-angle (90 degrees) clockwise, we will be facing East. If we face East, and turn in the opposite direction, we will be facing West. I am going to shout out a compass point, you need to jump and face that compass point.'

3. Shout out the compass points to take the children around in a clockwise direction i.e. N, E, S, W. Followed by moving in an anti-clockwise direction i.e. N, W, S, E. Then you can shout out directions in any order until the children are familiar with them.

Variations

- If your children find it difficult to remember the compass points you could display some large cards with the corresponding letters N, S, E, W on to begin with. They could be stuck to buildings, stakes in the ground, attached to chair backs or children could hold them.
- Why not use a magnetic compass initially to work out with the children which direction North is, and then highlight the other compass points. Alternatively, describe the front of the class as North.
- The number of compass points can be increased to 8, i.e. N, NE, E, SE, S, SW, W and NW. The children can jump to face these directions.
- Allow a child to take over the job of calling out the compass directions.

How Old is your Tree?

How Old is your Tree? is a practical Maths activity which encourages children to measure accurately and use a set formula for calculating a result.

Suitable for

KS1, KS2

Aims

- To choose and use suitable measuring instruments.
- To read scales and interpret numbers with increasing accuracy.

Resources

- Tape measures

What to do

1. Have the children sit outdoors in a circle. Ask some of the children to point out a tree and estimate how old it is. Discuss that it is difficult to work out the age of a tree without cutting it down to count the growth rings on the stump. When the stump is visible one growth ring accounts for one year of the tree's life.

2. Explain that there is another method to calculate a tree's age without cutting it down, and that to do this we need to measure the circumference of the tree at around one metre off the ground. Explain that circumference means the distance all the way around the tree trunk, if necessary.

3. Ask the children to choose an appropriate measuring instrument from a selection, which they will then take to their favourite nearby tree and measure its circumference. You could ask the children to make a note of the location of the tree and what the measurement was.

4. Once the children return to the circle they can begin to work out what the age of the tree was by completing one of the following calculations:

Metric method: Divide the measurement in cm by 2.5 to find the approximate age in years e.g. 61cm circumference divided by 2.5 = 24 years old.

Imperial method: 1 inch equals approximately 1 year of growth e.g. 2ft circumference = 24inches = 24 years old.

Variation

- Ask the children to measure all of the trees on the school site or in an area of woodland, collect all of the results in a table and ask the children to work out the average age of the trees on that site.

Leafy Lesson

> Leafy Lesson is a collection of Maths activities involving shape, space and measures which children will enjoy.

Suitable for

KS1, KS2

Aims

- To calculate the area and perimeter of shapes.
- To select and use appropriate calculation skills.

Resources

- Leaves
- String
- Pencils
- Paper with cm squares

What to do

1. Allow the children to collect 2 leaves each, 1 small and 1 large. Have the children discuss with a partner any differences between the leaves in terms of their shape, pattern and colour.

2. Discuss the main functions of leaves at a level appropriate to your class. (Photosynthesis and respiration.)

3. Ask the children to hold down their leaves using their fingertips and draw around the outlines using a pencil onto cm squared paper.

   Area: Discuss the meaning of the word area: the amount of surface a 2D shape covers, area is usually measured in square units such as cm^2.

   - Ask the children to estimate the surface area of their leaves.
   - Have the children calculate the area of their leaves by counting full cm squares, then partial squares.

- Encourage the children to develop their own way of finding the area of leaves by using their own system to record the number of full cm squares and partial squares, e.g. number each counted area, dot each counted square or mark portions which combine to make a full cm square with the same colour or pattern.
- Compare the estimates given to the real answer.
- Discuss the limitations of measuring a shape in this way.
- Explore the methods of calculating the area of rectangular or squared sections within the leaf by multiplying the length of one side by the other, rather than counting every individual square.

Perimeter: Discuss the meaning of the word perimeter: the total distance around the outside of a 2D shape.

- Discuss methods of calculating the perimeter of a square and a rectangle.
- Ask the children to estimate the perimeter of both of their leaves.
- Discuss the difficulties in calculating the perimeter of a leaf because of its lack of straight edges.
- Invite the children to think of a method of calculating the perimeter of their leaves. Suggest using string to mark out the outline of the leaf and measure the length of the string, if the children do not propose this method. The children may find it easier to work in pairs when trying to measure the perimeter of their leaves so that the string can be held down in more places, thus making the measurement more accurate.
- Discuss the limitations of measuring the perimeter in this way.

Variations

- Ask the children to estimate the total number of leaves on the tree that their leaf came from and calculate what the surface area of all of the leaves would be.
- Invite the children to investigate whether squaring off the edges to the nearest square on the leaf outline would help to give an accurate estimate on the perimeter of a leaf.

Ordering Nature

> Ordering Nature is a collection of practical Maths activities which encourage children to learn about measuring and ordering.

Suitable for

KS1, KS2

Aims

- To estimate the size of objects and order them by direct comparison using appropriate language.
- To choose and use suitable measuring instruments.
- To read scales and interpret numbers with increasing accuracy.

Resources

- Large collection of nature objects.
- Weighing scales
- Post-it notes (optional)

What to do

Have the children collect lots of nature objects to use, alternatively supply them with objects you have gathered. Choose one of the following activities depending upon the age and ability of your children, and have them work outside in pairs:

1. **Size** – the children select 5 or more objects and order them in a line from smallest to largest. Choose 5 different objects and order those from largest to smallest.

2. **Weight** – the children select 5 or more nature objects, weigh them using scales and order them in a line from lightest to heaviest. Choose 5 different objects, weigh and arrange them from heaviest to lightest.

The children could use Post-it notes to help keep a record of what the objects weighed.

3. **What's my order?** – the children order 5 or more objects in a line according to weight, length, size or any criteria they decide. They then change places with another partner group. Each has to work out how the other ordered their line of objects. The pairs explain how they think the other ordered their line and then discover if they were correct.

Variation

- Ask the children to choose 5 of the same object to be ordered according to their size or weight. This will call for some very accurate weighing and measuring.

Tall Trees

> Tall Trees is a practical Maths activity which encourages children to improvise and estimate when solving problems. The focus here is on measuring and multiplication.

Suitable for

KS1, KS2

Aims

- To understand multiplication as repeated addition.
- To use the correct language and vocabulary for measures.

Resources

- Art straws (for Straw Jumping activity)
- Scissors (optional)
- Metre sticks (for Hypsometer activity)

What to do

1. Ask 2 or 3 children to choose their favourite nearby trees. Invite the group to suggest which tree is the tallest and which is the smallest. Ask the children to estimate how tall the tallest tree is using appropriate units of measurement, and share their estimate with someone standing nearby.

2. Choose an appropriate method from the ones explained below to help calculate the height of the tallest tree. The first method (Straw Jumping) is more appropriate for younger children.

Straw Jumping

1. Invite the child who chose the tree to go and stand under it, once you have made sure that it is safe to do so. Have the other children

stand a distance back so that they can see the tree fully from bottom to top.

2. Each child needs to hold a piece of art straw at arm's length and tear or cut off a piece which is equal in size to the height of the child standing under the tree.

3. Now the children can begin to jump the straw up the tree, starting at the bottom, marking the place where the straw got to each time with their other hand outstretched. They should continue jumping up until they reach the top of the tree, not forgetting to count the number of steps as they go.

4. Once all of the children have finished straw jumping, the child standing under the tree should have her height measured, this measurement should be multiplied by the number of steps the children's straws took to give a reasonably accurate measurement for the height of the tree, e.g. 'Jack is 105cm tall, it took 7 steps to reach the top, therefore the tree is approximately 735cm or 7.35m tall.'

Hypsometer

1. Ask the children to stand back 5 metres from the tree and hold a metre stick 50cm from their eye.

2. Measure the height of the tree from bottom to top on the ruler. Each 10 cm will equal 1 metre of the tree's height. If the children are standing 10 metres back then each 10cm will equal 2 metres of the trees height, 15 metres back then 10cm will equal 3 metres etc.

3. Calculate the height and ask the children to compare results with others in the group.

Variation

- Ask the children to work in pairs and take turns at estimating and measuring the height of different trees using one of the methods described above.

Time Out

> Time Out is a Maths activity involving the estimating and measuring of time. There is a practical and active emphasis in these lesson ideas.

Suitable for

KS1, KS2

Aim

- To use units of time: seconds, minutes, hours, days, weeks, years and know the relationship between them.
- To select and use appropriate calculation skills.
- To make estimates and check results.

Resources

- Stopwatches
- Skipping ropes

What to do

1. Ask the children to estimate how long it will take to complete a list of set tasks. Record the estimates in a table. Here are some example tasks:

   - Run to the edge of the school field and back.
   - Complete 100 skips with a rope.
   - Throw and catch a ball 20 times with a partner.
   - Complete 40 star jumps.
   - Dribble a football 100m.
   - Pass a rugby ball along a line of 10 people.

2. Once they have estimated, invite the children to carry out the list of tasks and measure the time taken using a stopwatch. You may need

to demonstrate how to use a stopwatch accurately. The results should be recorded alongside the estimates.

3. Discuss the accuracy of the estimates when compared to the answers.

4. Set a second list of similar tasks, asking the children to estimate again beforehand. Measure using stopwatches to find out if their estimating ability has improved.

Variations

- Invite the children to think of their own ideas for the task list, estimate the time it would take, then carry out the tasks and measure them.
- Try letting the children count in their heads as a task is being completed and compare the time that they thought it took with the real measurement taken on a stopwatch. Are they counting seconds too quickly or too slowly? Discuss if there is anything they can do to help themselves estimate time more accurately.

Weather Analysis

Weather Analysis is a project which could be completed alongside Weather Report and its associated making activities (see pages 95–96). It is a handling data based project which will see the children develop their graph and chart-making skills and their ability to interpret data. This activity is aimed mainly at KS2 if allowing the children to work independently, although when working as a class led by an adult, some may be suitable for KS1 – also see the Variations for some differentiation ideas.

Suitable for

KS1, KS2

Aims

- To solve problems involving data.
- To draw conclusions from statistics and graphs.

Resources

- Graph paper
- Maths books/jotters
- Weather data – gained from completing a Weather Report project or data obtained from weather forecasts.
- Rulers
- Pencils and crayons
- Computer access (optional)

What to do

1. Have the children complete a Weather Report Project where they collect lots of data about rainfall, wind speed, wind direction, air temperature etc. Alternatively, ask the children to research the weather as homework for a fortnight or more, recording data to bring into school.

2. Explain to the children: 'We are going to be using the weather data which you have collected and using it to answer questions and make observations. At the moment, the data which you have collected is a mass of numbers which are difficult to interpret. We can improve this by using the data to make graphs and charts.'

3. Here are some suggestions for graphs and charts which the children could make. These could be hand-drawn or computer-generated:

Bar charts to show:
- Average daily temperature over 2 weeks.
- Daily rainfall.
- Most common wind direction daily.
- Average daily wind speed.

Line graphs to show:
- Highest daily temperature over 2 weeks.
- Lowest daily temperature over 2 weeks.
- Wind speed at 12.00pm over 2 weeks.
- Highest daily wind speed.

Pie charts to show:
- Proportion of days with no rain and some rain.
- Proportion of days with predominantly N, S, E or W wind direction.

4. Once the graphs and charts are created, you can set questions for the children to answer. Here are some examples:
- What was the most common wind direction in week 1?
- What was the highest daily wind speed?
- What was the lowest recorded temperature?
- What was the range in temperature over the 2 weeks?
- What do you predict the average daily rainfall to be in the following week?

Variations

- To simplify the activity you could create 2 or 3 bar graphs on the class whiteboard together and then ask the children to answer direct, one-step questions which you set, e.g. which day saw the most rainfall? Which was the hottest day? Which was the windiest day?
- Another option for differentiating the activity for lower ability or younger children would be to make pictograms using criteria such as number of days with rain vs. number of days without rain – these could be represented by a rain drop and a sunshine picture in the corresponding columns.
- To make the activity more challenging you could set the questions before making the graphs and charts, thus encouraging the children to decide on the appropriate way to display the necessary data and create their own graphs or charts to answer the questions.

Chapter 6
Music

Nature Music

Nature Music is a composition activity based on the theme of nature. The children will think of musical ways to recreate settings, creatures and movements.

Suitable for

KS1, KS2

Aims

- To improvise, developing rhythmic and melodic material when performing.
- To explore, choose, combine and organise musical ideas within musical structures.

Resources

- Class set of instruments
- Paper and pens/mini-whiteboards and pens

What to do

1. Have the children make a circle outdoors. Play a game such as 'Silent tambourine' where the children try to pass a tambourine around the circle making as little noise as possible.
2. Ask the children to discuss with a partner what sounds they think of when you tell them the theme for the compositions they will be making. Some theme examples for the Nature Music compositions are: birds/insects/seasons/weather etc.
3. Ask the children to think of ways in which they could make some of these nature sounds using instruments. Keep the instruments in the middle of the circle and invite any children who have particularly good suggestions to demonstrate their idea.

4. Organise the children into small groups for composing. Whilst you distribute the instruments, instruct the children to assign some roles within their groups such as: a conductor (to lead the group, tell them when to join in, start, stop and how loud to play   using hand gestures) a scribe (to record the composition in some way using a grid, a picture or some form of simple notation for the others to follow) and an announcer (to announce the title of the piece of music and explain a little about it before the piece is performed later on).

5. Once they have allocated roles, allow the children plenty of time to compose and rehearse. You might want to structure the session giving the children 10 minutes to develop an introduction, 15 minutes for a main section and 10 minutes for an ending. You could suggest ideas to any struggling groups such as: a long, slow cymbal roll to symbolise sunrise in the introduction/a triangle tapping out a repeated rhythm to represent a bird pecking in the middle section etc.

6. Invite the others to listen and think of evaluative comments while each group performs its composition.

Variations

- Why not listen to, and evaluate some examples of music inspired by nature before you begin the composition session? Try Vivaldi, *The Four Seasons*/Groove Armada, *At the River*/Saint-Saëns, *Carnival of the Animals*.
- You could allow the children to select their own theme based on nature for their group compositions.

Shaker Maker

Shaker Maker is a simple making activity which sees the children use nature objects to create interesting sounds.

Suitable for

KS1, KS2

Aims

- To improvise, developing rhythmic and melodic material when performing.
- To use nature objects to create musical instruments.

Resources

- Empty plastic bottles/other empty, clean and sealable containers
- Scissors
- Parcel tape
- Selection of nature/natural objects

What to do

1. Have the children choose a bottle/container each and decide which nature objects they will choose to fill it.
2. Some ideas for shaker materials: acorns/conkers/pebbles/gravel/broken up twigs/berries/seeds/dead leaves.
3. Only fill the bottles/containers half full to allow space to shake them properly.
4. Put the cap back on the bottle and wrap tape around to secure it.
5. Some children could try making shakers using only one type of object to fill them; others could try a combination of different objects in a bottle and compare the sounds made.

6. Ask the children to work in small groups and experiment with the kind of sounds and rhythms they can create with their shakers.

Variations

- Why not invite the children to think of other ways in which they can use nature objects to make music.
- You could create a class composition by dividing the children into groups and making a 'Beat It' grid, where a shaded chart shows the children on which beats of the bar they should play their instrument.

Beat It! Grid Example

Acorn shakers	1	2	3	4
Pebble shakers	1	2	3	4
Twig shakers	1	2	3	4

Sound Walk

> Sound Walk is a great activity which encourages the development of listening skills and encourages children's creativity when recreating sounds.

Suitable for

KS1, KS2

Aims

- To develop listening and recording skills.
- To encourage improvisation with sounds and exploration of timbre (tone colour/quality).
- To respond to non-musical starting points.

Resources

- Paper, pencils and clipboards
- Class set of instruments
- Portable tape recorder/dictaphone/laptop and microphone (optional)

What to do

1. Lead the children on a walk around a pre-determined route. This could be inside in the school grounds, in a local woodland or in a playground.

2. Choose appropriate places on the route for the children to stop and listen for a minute in silence. The children record on their paper any sounds which they can hear at each location. The paper can be divided up into sections and numbered/labelled as to the location of each stop on the sound walk. The children can note down the sounds heard using a combination of written descriptions and pictures. You could also record the sounds using a portable digital recorder, tape dictaphone or laptop.

3. Return to school and work in groups to recreate the stages of the sound walk using instruments, voices and body percussion. This can be organised by asking individual groups to recreate one part of the sound walk and then the groups can perform their compositions in turn to replicate the stages of the sound walk. Alternatively, all groups can be asked to recreate the whole sound walk.

4. The class performance of the sound walk can be tape recorded, then listened to by the children and compared to the sound recordings taken on the sound walk.

Chapter 7
PSHE & Citizenship

All Aboard

All Aboard is a simple game which can be played outside with your class. The children will enjoy this team game and realise that they will have to work together if they are going to succeed.

Suitable for

KS1, KS2

Aim

- To develop relationships through work and play.

Resources

- 2 blankets/tarpaulins/dustsheets/duvet covers or bed-sheets
- Whistle

What to do

1. Divide the class into 2 equal teams. Have the 2 teams stand on separate blankets of the same size.
2. Tell the children that they will need to turn the sheet completely over, but they mustn't touch the ground when doing so.
3. If anyone does touch the ground when turning the sheet over, then their team has to start again.
4. Encourage the children to discuss a strategy before blowing a whistle to start the game.
5. The winning team is the first to have everyone standing on the other side of the blanket.
6. Play the game 3 times, the overall winning team gets a reward.

Variation

- Make the game more difficult by folding the blankets in half. Then fold again if the children complete the challenge.

Blindfold Journeys

Blindfold Journeys are brilliant fun. When children wear a blindfold they are forced to focus on their other senses and trust those in control. Here are 5 blindfold activities to try.

Suitable for

KS1, KS2

Aims

- To develop relationships through work and play.
- To listen to other people and play and work cooperatively.

Resources

- Blindfolds
- Rope

What to do

When using blindfolds always remind children of the safety implications, e.g. no running and act responsibly when leading. The following games can be completed in any order:

1. **Blindfold Circle**. Each child wears a blindfold and sits outdoors in a circle. Objects are passed around the group without talking. Once the object has made it around the circle, the children can suggest what they thought the object might have been. Try using: a pine cone, an orange, a pebble, a leaf etc.

2. **Blindfold Partners**. Pairs of children take turns to lead whilst the other wears a blindfold. The blindfolded child is led carefully on a journey which stops at certain points to experience sensations using the senses such as smelling a flower or herbs, touching a tree trunk, listening to birds.

3. Rope Route. The children all wear blindfolds and are led to a route which is marked by a fixed rope that journeys around an interesting area. The children should stay on one side of the rope and keep contact with it at all times. The children should start the rope route at intervals of 30 seconds so that there are no collisions. You could place obstacles along the route, but make sure that someone is able to supervise the children as they encounter each obstacle. You may also need a helper at the end of the route to tell the children that they have finished.

4. Blind Snakes. Groups of 5 children are blindfolded except for the person at the front of the line. They place their hands on the shoulders of the child in front of them and the leader takes them on a journey to a new location. The children remove their blindfolds and try to work out the route they took to get to the new location. A new leader then takes over for a new journey.

5. Blindfold Guessing. Pairs or small groups of blindfolded children are led to a new location where they stop and use their remaining senses to investigate the environment. The leader returns the blindfolded children to the original starting point. The children remove their blindfolds and try to guess the location they were taken to.

Journey Stick

A Journey Stick is literally a stick which tells the story of a journey. This is a great activity which really focuses children upon the route they have taken and the things they have seen when walking outdoors.

Suitable for

KS1, KS2

Aims

- To make a journey stick of a walk/route.
- To be able to retell and explain a journey.

Resources

- Sticks
- Nature objects
- Wool/string/thread/tape

What to do

1. Lead the children on a circular walk in a suitable location such as a woodland or field etc.

2. Ask each child to find a stick to use to represent their journey. You may wish to provide sticks rather than allowing the children to find them. Remind the children about the safety implications of carrying sticks around.

3. As the children travel along the route they gather nature objects which interest them, or objects which signify a certain stage of the journey and they attach them to their stick using wool or string. The stick should show a linear progression of the journey, i.e. objects attached at the end of the journey should be at the far end of the journey stick,

those objects attached at the beginning of the journey should be at the base close to the hand.

4. The children should follow your guidelines on what objects are safe/acceptable to attach, e.g. are they allowed to pick living leaves or grasses in the area?

5. Once the journey is complete, have the children work in small groups to retell their story using their journey stick as a prompt.

Variations

- Allow the children to gather their journey stick objects independently in an area with set boundaries, rather than leading a circular walk; this will allow each journey to be unique and make the retelling more interesting for the audience, but it can be more challenging to supervise.
- You could encourage less confident children to tell their journey stick story to a partner rather than to a group.
- Try asking children to choose different coloured wool to symbolise their emotions/feelings as well as the stages and experiences of the journey.
- Try turning the journey sticks into a pictorial map of the walk.

Outdoor Circle Games

> Outdoor Circle Games is a collection of circle time activities which lend themselves to being done outdoors.

Suitable for

KS1, KS2

Aims

- To help children to learn the names of all of their classmates.
- To develop the attitude of teamwork.
- To recognise their worth as individuals by identifying positive things about themselves.

Resources

- Soft football

What to do

Have the children sit in a circle. Introduce/discuss the class circle time rules.

Circle time rules:

- Listen to each other
- Respect other people's ideas
- Wait your turn and don't interrupt
- Speak when you have the ball or talking object
- Pass if you want to

Play the following outdoor circle games in any order:

1. **Roller Ball.** Explain to the children: 'You need to sit with your legs outstretched, you might want to put your hands out behind you for stability, the ball needs to travel all the way around the circle without

touching the floor. You are only allowed to use your legs. You need to work as a team to stop the ball from touching the floor.'

Before starting the game, you may wish to lead a few leg stretching exercises such as: pointing toes away and then towards you or raising both legs off the ground together and slowly lowering them.

Once the game starts, you can choose whether to restart the game when the ball touches the floor, or to carry on from the point where it fell.

2. **I think you're great.** Explain to the children: 'I am going to roll the ball to someone in the circle; I will then say 'I think you're great because ...,' and then I will give a reason why. The reason I give could be: something I like about that person, something they have done which impressed me, something kind which they did for me, or something which I know that they are good at. Roll the ball to a child and say 'I think you're great because ...' (giving a reason why), that child then rolls the ball to another child and repeats the phrase 'I think you're great because ...'

The game can continue whilst you encourage children to make sure that everyone is being included. You may wish to ask children to roll the ball to children who have not yet been chosen.

The game concludes when everyone has paid and received a compliment. A discussion can then take place to describe how it felt to give and receive a compliment.

3. **Name Game.** Explain to the children: 'When you receive the ball, say your name loudly and clearly, and then pass the ball onto the next person in the circle.'

Once all children have had their turn, explain: 'This time you need to say your name and tell everyone something that you like. This could be a hobby, interest, favourite lesson or even your favourite food.'

Once all children have had their turn, a discussion can take place about how everyone in the class is unique, how it is good to find out things about each other and important to value the differences between us.

Parachute Ball Games

Parachute Games are great fun to play for children of all ages. The children need to cooperate and work as a team to be successful. It is important to remind children of your safety rules before taking the parachute out, e.g. do not make physical contact with anybody if moving under the parachute, remove any jewellery etc.

Suitable for

KS1, KS2

Aims

- To encourage the attitudes of teamwork and cooperation.
- To plan, use and adapt strategies.
- To improve coordination.

Resources

- Parachute and large clear space outdoors
- Selection of balls

What to do

1. Have the children stand in a circle. You should remind the class of the parachute safety rules before unrolling the parachute.
2. The following games can be played in any order:

   A. Flip. All children hold the edge of the parachute. Roll a ball into the centre. The aim is to make the ball rise up into the air and flip off the parachute. The children will need to experiment with different techniques as a team to make these things happen. You could add more balls, or different sized balls. If multiple balls are added, a time limit can be set to try and flip all of the balls off the parachute.

B. **Flip Catch**. Half of the children hold the edge of the parachute whilst the others stand around the edge of the parachute. Roll a ball into the middle of the parachute. The aim is to flip the ball out of the parachute to be caught by one of the children standing around the edge. When a child catches the ball, they can join the children in holding the edge of the parachute.

C. **Rollercoaster**. All children hold the edge of the parachute. Place the ball in front of one child. The aim is to make the ball travel all the way around the edge of parachute. This game can be played sitting or standing, and the children may require several attempts before discovering how to accomplish the aim.

D. **Ball Keeper**. Some children stand or crouch under the parachute while the others hold the edge of the parachute up at chest height. Roll several balls onto the parachute. The aim for children under the parachute is to knock the balls off the parachute. The aim for the children holding the edge is to keep the balls on the parachute.

Variation

- Try using bean bags instead of balls, this can make some of the games easier to play.

Parachute Movement Games

Parachute Games are great fun to play for children of all ages. The children need to cooperate and work as a team to be successful. It is important to remind children of your safety rules before taking the parachute out, e.g. do not make physical contact with anybody if moving under the parachute, remove any jewellery etc.

Suitable for

KS1, KS2

Aims

- To encourage the attitudes of teamwork and cooperation.
- To plan, use and adapt strategies.
- To improve coordination.

Resources

- Parachute and a large clear space outdoors

What to do

1. Invite the children to stand in a circle. Remind the class of the parachute rules before unrolling the parachute.
2. The following games can be played in any order:
   A. **Birthdays**. The children practise lifting the parachute up into the air as a team, holding the edge above their head. Call out the name of a month when the parachute is on the way up, any child with a birthday in that month goes under the parachute and moves into an empty space around the edge before the parachute falls. This type of game can be played by giving each child a number, colour or team, rather than using months as the signal to

move. You can ask just the boys or the girls to change places, or the instruction all change can be given; always remind children to be careful to avoid collisions.

B. **Mexican Wave.** The children crouch whilst holding the edge of the parachute. Choose one child to stand quickly to begin a Mexican wave. The children jump up one by one in a clockwise direction to create the effect.

C. **Wave Maker.** All children sit holding the edge of the parachute. Tell the children that they are going to create the story of a storm. Ask the children to make gentle ripples on the surface by making small movements. This can then build up into huge crashing waves with large movements. A story about a storm could be read/made up in which the children need to perform the correct movements at the appropriate time.

D. **Circus Tent.** The children hold the edge of the parachute, stand and lift it above their heads. The aim is for the children to bring the parachute behind their heads and down until they can sit on the piece which they were holding. This creates a 'circus tent', one child can be chosen to go to the centre of the parachute to support it with their head to act as a tent pole! This provides an unusual and atmospheric feel for discussions or storytelling.

E. **Shark.** The children sit with their legs outstretched under the parachute whilst holding the edge. The children make small waves by moving the edge up and down gently. One child is chosen to go under the parachute to become the shark, they move around and then tap one child on the leg. This child then goes under the parachute to become the shark, and the old shark takes their place around the edge. You can allow more than one shark to be under the parachute so long as the children are very careful not to make physical contact with each other.

Pass the Stick

Pass the Stick is a simple game which can be played outside with your class. The children will enjoy this team game and realise that they will have to work together if they are going to succeed.

Suitable for

KS1, KS2

Aim

• To develop relationships through work and play.

Resources

• 2 small sticks or other nature objects which can be passed along a line

What to do

1. Divide the class into 2 equal teams. Have the 2 teams stand opposite one another in a line facing each other.
2. Tell the children to hold hands with the person standing next to them. They are not allowed to let go of hands until the game has finished.
3. The challenge is to pass a stick all the way down the line without it dropping to the ground.
4. You can start the game by giving the sticks to the first person in each of the lines at the same time.
5. If the stick falls to the ground, then it has to be picked up with hands still held together.
6. Play the game 5 times, the overall winning team gets a reward.

Variations

- Make the game more difficult by stating that if the stick falls to the ground, then it has to start at the beginning of the line again.
- Try asking the children to cross their arms over before taking the hand of the person next to them.
- How about having 2 sticks travelling in opposite directions along the line.
- You could divide the children into 4 equal teams if you have a large class.
- Challenge the children to create new variations on this simple game.

The Memory Game

The Memory Game is an enjoyable challenge with four variations to try. The basic principal is that the children have one minute to try to remember a group of nature objects.

Suitable for

KS1, KS2

Aims

- To develop short-term memory skills.
- To learn the names of common nature objects.

Resources

- Selection of 10 to 20 nature objects
- Tray
- Towel/paper to cover
- Small whiteboards/paper for children

What to do

1. Place a selection of 10 to 20 nature objects outdoors on a tray or on the ground and cover them up with a towel e.g. acorn, pebble, driftwood, snail shell, apple etc.
2. **Explain to the children**. 'You will have one minute to try and remember as many of the items under the towel as you can. Once the minute is up, I will cover the items up again.'
3. **Write it down**. The children write a list of as many objects as they can remember within a set time limit. The child who remembers the most is the winner.
4. **Find it**. The children try to find as many of the objects from the tray as they can in a set area such as the school field. They could collect the

objects in a bag in a set time limit. The child/team with the most correct objects wins.

5. **Draw it**. The children have a set time limit to draw as many of the objects as they can remember. You can let them use a numbered grid with one space for each new drawing. The child with the most correct drawings wins.

6. **Name it**. The children have 30 seconds to name out loud as many of the objects from the tray as they can without repeating any. The child who names the most correctly is the winner.

Variations

- Why not teach the children some memory techniques such as visualisation, chaining or acrostics before playing the game?
- You could award a prize for the child who gets the most correct items.
- Try asking a child to choose the objects and lead the game.
- A variation of this game is to show the items for one minute, then cover and remove one or more items from the tray. Reveal the items again, and the winner is the first child to work out what is missing.
- You can make the game easier or harder by using fewer or more items on the tray and by increasing or decreasing the viewing times.

Outdoor Improvements

> Outdoor Improvements allows the children to take responsibility for developing an area of the school grounds which needs improvement.

Suitable for

KS2

Aim

- To face new challenges positively by collecting information, looking for help, making responsible choices and taking action.

Resources

- Dependent upon the type of project undertaken

What to do

1. Identify an area of the school grounds which is in need of improvement.

2. Explain to the children that they are going to be given responsibility for this location and that they will need to decide what they are going to do with it.

3. Options for regenerating an area could be an outdoor art gallery, to create seating, to make a play space, to plant a vegetable garden, to make a sensory garden or to build a nature area etc. You may wish to give the children a list of suitable options and let them decide on one.

4. Help the children to allocate areas of research based upon the kind of project they are undertaking. Research could include using any or all of the following techniques: use the internet, books, questionnaires, ask parents and talk to professionals.

5. Assist the children in making a budget plan and a projected timescale based on their research. You may want the children to develop ideas for fundraising to finance the project; alternatively the children could approach the school council, the head teacher, parents associations or outside bodies for financial help.

6. Once the funds are in place, the children can oversee the ordering and purchasing of any items required, and begin work on the transformation.

7. Why not allow the children to host an opening event to which parents, children, governors and the local press are invited.

8. When the project is complete, the children can prepare a presentation to explain their project to the rest of the school.

Variations

- Structure the project as much or as little as you need to depending upon the ability of your children.
- A project of this kind has so many cross-curricular implications – why not devote a whole week to it?

Chapter 8
Science

Acorn Planting

Acorn Planting is a practical activity where the children work through several stages with the goal of growing oak seedlings.

Suitable for

KS1, KS2

Aims

- To understand that seeds grow into plants.
- To recognise that plants need light and water to grow.

Resources

- Acorns (collected by the children)
- Bucket of water
- Small plant pots/plastic cups
- Compost
- Rulers

What to do

1. Lead a visit to a woodland location with plenty of oak trees. Show the children an acorn, discuss which tree it comes from and the fact that it is a seed.

2. Send the children in pairs to collect acorns from the floor in a designated area. Explain that they may have to look under fallen leaves to find acorns – remind the children about safety when handling nature objects i.e. do not put nature objects or your hands in your mouth after handling them, wash your hands before eating etc.

3. Once each pair has filled their plant pot/plastic cup with acorns have them return to you for the next stage. Discuss which creatures

may have also been hunting for acorns in the woodland whilst you wait for all of the pairs to return.

4. The children take turns to do a float/sink test by dropping their acorns into a bucket of water. The ones which float should be discarded, and the ones which sink should be put back into the pot/cup and taken back to school.

5. Once back at school, plant the acorns in compost and water them regularly. Be aware that acorns can take several weeks to germinate.

6. Measure the growth of the seedlings using a ruler.

Variations

- Wait until the seedlings are a healthy size and plant them outside.
- Allow the children to take their seedlings home to look after them and return after a month to see whose has grown the best.
- Experiment by planting the acorns in different directions, some with the cap up, down or sideways.
- Allow the children to collect different seeds such as beech or chestnut and then separate the acorns out.

Animal Partners

Animal Partners is a fun and active game where the children act as a specific animal whilst being on the lookout for their animal partner.

Suitable for

KS1, KS2

Aims

- To recognise and compare the behaviour of animals.
- To use actions to convey situations and characteristics.

Resources

- Pairs of animal name cards
- Bag/hat to hold cards
- Whistle

What to do

1. Count the number of children taking part and add that number of animal name cards to the bag. The animal cards should be in pairs, or threes: e.g. 2 × lion/2 × elephant/2 × dog/3 × snake.

2. Invite each child to pick a card from the bag, look at their card in secret and place it in their pocket. When a child takes a card they should go and stand in a space outdoors in a designated game area. Once all have taken a card the game can begin.

3. The children need to act as the animal on their card using their bodies only to simulate the movement, shape and habits of the animal. They are not allowed to make any noises or talk. At the same time the children should be on the lookout for another child/children who are acting out the same animal as themselves. If they suspect

they have found their partner animal, then they should stand
together and carry on their actions until you blow a whistle.

4. When the whistle blows the children take out their cards and show
it to their partner to find out if they were a correct pair.

5. Return the cards to the bag and the game can begin again.

Variations

- With a larger class you could try adding 4 or 5 of the same animal cards to
the bag.
- Try allowing the children to make animal noises to begin with if they find the
actions only version too difficult.

Animal Tracks

Animal Tracks is an investigative activity where the children try to identify an animal by looking at its tracks. Take a look at the 'Variations' for some fun follow up games/alternatives.

Suitable for

KS1, KS2

Aims

- To recognise and compare the tracks of animals.
- To find out about the different kinds of animals in the local environment.

Resources

- Animal tracks reference cards
- Animal tracks flash cards
- Sticks
- Digital camera (optional)
- Clay (optional)

What to do

1. Lead a visit to a woodland location or somewhere that you know the children will be able to find animal tracks.

2. Hand out animal tracks reference cards (these can be purchased ready-made or downloaded from the internet) and invite the children to search in a designated area for any tracks which they can find. When they find a track they should try and identify it, then share their discovery with you. Alternatively have the children walk slowly along a route in small groups with a leader, looking for tracks together and stopping to identify them when any are found.

3. Take close-up photographs of any tracks found and print these out back at school. Mount the photos on a display created by the children with a fact file about the animal.

4. Discuss the differences between the animal tracks and the reasons why they might be that way.

Variations

- Use a sandpit and water, a muddy area or clay to make animal tracks using sticks. The children work in pairs, taking turns to draw and identify animal tracks that the other has made using a stick.
- Make individual flash cards showing animal tracks on the one side with the name of the animal on the other. Play a recognition game in teams where each time a team identifies a track correctly they get a point, and if they cannot identify it, then the next team gets to guess and steal the point.

Bird's Nest

Bird's Nest is a practical activity, ideal for younger children, where they attempt to build their own nest.

Suitable for

KS1, KS2

Aims

- To relate life processes to animals found in the local environment.
- To understand that animals produce offspring which will grow into adults.

Resources

- A bird's nest
- Grass, twigs, leaves etc.

What to do

1. Lead the children on a walk to a location where you know there is a bird's nest.

2. Explain that the children will need to be quiet so as not to scare the birds. Discuss what a bird's nest is for and the reasons why they are built in places off the ground.

3. Ask the children what kind of things a bird might use to make its nest with.

4. Set the children a challenge of making a bird's nest themselves using grass, twigs, leaves and mud etc. The nest will need to hold one egg safely.

5. Allow the children to make and test their nest.

Variations

- Try placing the children's nests in the low branches of a tree.
- You could use pine cones or chocolate eggs to simulate a bird's egg in the nest.

Learning about Leaves

> Learning about Leaves is a set of simple activities which help children to learn about leaves and the tress from which they come.

Suitable for

KS1, KS2

Aims

- To learn how to identify different leaves.
- To learn the names of common trees found in the local environment.
- To learn the names of different leaf parts and understand their function.

Resources

- Tree and leaf identification cards/sheets/books (these can be purchased or downloaded and printed from the internet)
- Collection of leaves – one per child
- Leaf name cards
- Leaf picture cards

What to do

Have the children sit in a circle outdoors. Hand out a leaf to each child and discuss the following parts of a leaf:

Blade – the flat surface of a leaf
Stalk/Petiole – the part which joins the leaf to the plant/tree
Margin – the edge of the leaf, this can be entire, lobed or toothed
Vein – the lines which run from the tip and edge
Apex – the tip of the leaf.

*Why not discuss with older children what each part of the leaf does and why/how?

Play the following games in the order they are written:

1. **Finding.** The children work in pairs to find leaves and identify them using leaf identification pictures/cards/field guides. The children choose three leaves that they have found and bring those back to the circle having learned their names. The children show their leaves to the others in the circle.

2. **Matching.** Pairs of children are given 3 or more leaf picture cards and 3 matching leaf name cards, they have a set time to match the correct picture to the correct leaf name using identification cards or field guides to help. Try repeating the game by mixing the leaf picture and name cards up and taking away the identification cards/field guides. The children now try to match them together from memory.

3. **Learning.** Children are given a selection of leaves from the local environment either in groups, or individually. The children have to identify the leaves and score a point for each one they name correctly.

Variation

• Try some matching or learning games with seeds as well as leaves.

Planting and Growing

What follows is a selection of practical activities which focus on plants and their functions. The children will enjoy planting, examining and observing. One of the most rewarding experiences for children is to watch a plant grow from a seed which they have sown and then be able to eat it.

Suitable for

KS1, KS2

Aims

- To understand that seeds grow into flowering plants.
- To find out about the different kinds of plants and animals in the local environment.
- To recognise that the life processes common to plants include growth, nutrition and reproduction.
- To recognise and name the leaf, flower, stem and root of flowering plants.
- To understand that it is important to test ideas using evidence from observation and measurement.
- To use observations and data to draw conclusions.

Resources

Depending upon the activity chosen you may need:
- Plant pots or suitable containers
- Soil/potting compost
- Black sugar paper
- Various seeds
- Tomato plants
- Labels
- Clipboards
- Watering can

What to do

Choose from the following list of activities ones which are suitable for the ability level of your children. Always remind children to wash their hands after handling plants, leaves or soil.

A. Plant survey. Allow the children to explore the school grounds or local area (with appropriate supervision), they should make sketches and notes about the different types of plants and trees which they find. The children can then share their findings with the class and begin to identify the diversity of plants species and the similarities and differences between them.

B. Growing from seed. Children love to see plants grow from seeds. Use plastic cups or any suitable pot for growing the seeds and remember to get the children to label the pots with their names. You might need to start them off on a sunny windowsill inside the classroom, then transplant them outdoors. Sunflower seeds are ideal for this purpose. Encourage the children to look after their plant by watering it and choosing a good location for it. You could measure the plants on a daily or weekly basis and record the data.

C. Water. Children will quickly learn that plants need water to survive if they set up an indoor group experiment with two young tomato plants, one which will be watered and the other not. Decide with the children how you are going to make the test fair, i.e. using the same sized plant and pot, putting the plants in the same location, using the same amount of soil etc. Encourage the children to make predictions on what they think will happen. It may take up to a week before the plant with no water begins to show a noticeable difference. Remember to clearly label the plant which is to have no water, and emphasise that the other plant must not be over-watered. Transplant the healthy plant outdoors at the appropriate time, feed and water regularly and harvest the tomatoes.

D. Light. Compare the effects of light upon plants by using young tomato plants in the same way as activity C (Water). This time both plants should receive equal water, but one should be completely covered. An easy way of doing this is to make cone shapes using two layers of black sugar paper or card. Transplant the healthy plant outdoors at the appropriate time.

E. Temperature. Examine the effects of temperature upon plants by using tomato plants in the same way as Activities C and D. This time one of the plants should be kept in a fridge whilst the other stays at room temperature.

F. Nutrients. This investigation will demonstrate that plants need nutrients (minerals) to grow well. The children should plant broad bean seeds in a variety of growing materials such as sand, grit, different soils (you could ask the children to bring in soil from their garden), sawdust and cotton wool etc. Decide with the children how the test will be kept fair i.e. same location, same water, same sized pot etc. Discuss how the children are going to judge the healthiness of the plants and how they are going to record their data before and during the investigation. Once the plants show obvious differences, you should discuss the reasons why and compare the results to the children's predictions.

G. Plant parts. Collect a variety of plants and flowers for the children to examine. Invite the children to draw and label any parts of the plants which they know the names and functions of. Collect the children's ideas and go on to correct any misconceptions. Explain the functions of leaves, roots, stems and flowers at an appropriate level for your children's ability. Repeat the drawing and labelling activity as an assessment opportunity.

H. Plants for food. To show the process of plants being grown for food why not grow plants such as herbs or vegetables from seed at school. This is a long-term project which requires careful planning and maintenance, but the learning and sense of satisfaction which the children will get from eating their own produce will more than justify the effort. There are many plants suitable for this project including carrots, peas, spinach, coriander, tomatoes etc. Why not let the children choose what it is they would like to grow, and cultivate a selection by sowing seeds, transplanting them and harvesting. If there is a lack of suitable space at school, then try approaching the nearest allotment. There are numerous organisations which offer advice and support. The children could plan to incorporate their produce into a meal which could be prepared for a school dinner.

Sweep Net

Sweep Net is an enjoyable way of letting children explore and collect small creatures found on plants. A sweep net is a large wooden handle with a cone shaped net attached to a circular frame on the end.

Suitable for

KS1, KS2

Aim

- To learn about the animals found in different habitats.

Resources

- Sweep nets
- Bug viewers
- Field guides/mini-beast identification cards

What to do

1. Gather the children outside and explain that in groups they are going to be using sweep nets to collect small creatures.

2. Demonstrate how to carry and use a sweep net safely by sweeping it quickly but gently through low vegetation or on the edge of a hedge. The net is then examined and any interesting creatures can be carefully transferred to a bug viewer or an observation tank.

3. Ask the children to take turns using the sweep net and collect as many different creatures as they can.

4. Allow the children to record their findings using labelled drawings. You might wish to use field guides or the internet to help identify the creatures.

5. Safely return the creatures to where they were collected from.

Variations

- Try having groups sweep net in different areas, then compare the results.
- Why not have different groups collecting creatures in a variety of ways and compare/share their findings at the end of the session, e.g. one group using a sweep net, one group pond dipping, one group holding a white sheet under a safe low tree branch and shaking it to see what falls out etc.
- See companion website for details of where to buy sweep nets and other useful resources.

What am I?

What am I? is an enjoyable game for children to play in a small or large group. They will ask questions to work out their animal identity.

Suitable for

KS1, KS2

Aims

- To recognise and compare the bodies of animals.
- To find out about the different kinds of animals in the local environment.

Resources

- Selection of animal picture cards in a bag for each group (these are best laminated)
- Card strip headbands with slots cut at the front

What to do

1. The children sit or stand in circles wearing a card headband. One child holds the bag of pictures.
2. The child with the bag chooses a picture card and places it into the headband of the child next to them in the circle without that child seeing the animal on the card.
3. The card wearer then has 10 questions to ask the group in order to work out their animal identity.
4. The group can only reply to questions with 'Yes/No/Maybe.'
5. If a child hasn't guessed correctly within 10 questions then the group can tell them what their animal identity is.
6. The game continues until all children are wearing an animal card in their headbands.

Variations

- The child asking the questions could choose which group member they wish to answer their question by pointing or saying their name before asking.
- You may wish to explore some examples of 'good' questions with the children before playing the game: 'Am I a mammal?' 'Have I got 4 legs?' 'Do I eat insects?' 'Do I have fur?'
- You could limit the animal cards to animals which are found in the local environment, animals from the rainforest, predators or reptiles etc.
- With younger children you could teach them about the animals on their cards before playing the game.
- The children could make their own animal cards and decorate their own headbands.
- You could play the game each week as part of an outdoor lesson, and keep adding new animal cards to the bags each time.

What's Underneath?

What's Underneath is a practical investigative activity where children lift objects to discover what is underneath them.

Suitable for

KS1, KS2

Aim

- To learn about the animals found in different habitats.

Resources

- Logs/branches, large stones/rocks
- Paper, clipboards and pencils
- Digital camera (optional)
- Bug viewers (optional)

What to do

1. Gather the children outside and explain that in groups they are going to place a log/branch or a large stone/rock in a position on the school field or in a nature area. The object needs to be carried safely and it will be left in the same position overnight.

2. Ask the children to predict what they will find under the object when they lift it on the following day. Have the children write or draw their predictions on one half of a piece of paper.

3. The following day, return to the logs/stones in groups and carefully lift them to see what creatures are underneath. The children could take a close-up photograph of the results.

4. Have the children draw and list what they found, and use field guides to help identify any unfamiliar creatures.

5. Discuss the reasons why the creatures/mini-beasts were found underneath the objects.

Variations

- Try looking underneath fallen logs or stones when out on a walk with your children.
- Investigate what would happen if the log or stone was left for a week before it was turned over.
- How about collecting some of the mini-beasts found and studying them in more detail using bug viewers.

Index of activities

Name of activity	KS1	KS2	Instant Gems*	Page
Nature Sculptures	✓	✓		44
Nature Treasure Hunt	✓	✓		87
Ordering Nature	✓	✓		114
Orienteering	✓	✓		91
Outdoor Chair	✓	✓		46
Outdoor Circle Games	✓	✓	✓	140
Outdoor Classroom	✓	✓		4
Outdoor Improvements		✓		150
Outdoor Kit Bag	✓	✓		6
Outdoor Patterns	✓		✓	104
Outdoor Poetry	✓	✓	✓	72
Outdoor Storytime	✓	✓		74
Parachute Ball Games	✓	✓	✓	142
Parachute Movement Games	✓	✓	✓	144
Pass the Stick	✓	✓	✓	146
Planting and Growing	✓	✓		164
Post It	✓	✓		77
Rain Gauge	✓	✓		93
Seasons Pictures	✓	✓	✓	49
Shaker Maker	✓	✓		128
Shelter Making	✓	✓✓		51
Sound Walk	✓	✓		130
Sticky Pictures	✓	✓		54
Sweep Net	✓	✓		167
Tall Trees	✓	✓		116
Teaching Outdoors Tips	✓	✓		8
The Big Picture	✓	✓		57
The Countryside Rules	✓	✓	✓	10
The Memory Game	✓	✓		148
Time Out	✓	✓✓		118
Weather Analysis	✓	✓		120

*Instant Gems are off-the-shelf activities which require little or no preparation.

Classroom Gems

Innovative resources, inspiring creativity across the school curriculum

Designed with busy teachers in mind, the Classroom Gems series draws together an extensive selection of practical, tried-and-tested, off-the-shelf ideas, games and activities, guaranteed to transform any lesson or classroom in an instant.

© 2008 Paperback 336pp
ISBN: 9781405873925

© 2008 Paperback 312pp
ISBN: 9781405859455

© 2009 Paperback 216pp
ISBN: 9781408220382

© 2009 Paperback 232pp
ISBN: 9781408225578

© 2009 Paperback 392pp
ISBN: 9781408223208

© 2009 Paperback 320pp
ISBN: 9781408228098

© 2009 Paperback 312pp
ISBN: 9781408223260

© 2009 Paperback 352pp
ISBN: 9781408223291

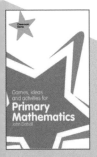

'Easily navigable, allowing teachers to choose the right activity quickly and easily, these invaluable resources are guaranteed to save time and are a must-have tool to plan, prepare and deliver first-rate lessons'

© 2009 Paperback 384pp
ISBN: 9781408224359